The Structure of
Accounting Theory

To My Parents

The Structure of Accounting Theory

S. C. Yu

A University of Florida Book

The University Presses of Florida
Gainesville / 1976

Library of Congress Cataloging in Publication Data

Yu, Shih Cheng, 1921–
    The structure of accounting theory.

    Includes index.
    1. Accounting. I Title.
HP5601.F55   657'.08s   76–10355
ISBN 0–8130–0538–8

Contents

1 Introduction

With the exceptions of logic and mathematics, all disciplines are, by and large, empirical in nature, and an empirical discipline is one that deals with a specified class of phenomena of the existential world (i.e., a segment of the total environment) in terms of explanation and prediction. To be operational, each empirical discipline needs a foundation upon which it can rest and a conceptual framework within which it can explain and predict the specified class of events. The term "discipline" in this context is defined as a branch of systematized learning; it is governed by a set of formal rules regulating the process of knowledge acquisition. Since accounting is concerned with classifying, depicting, summarizing, and interpreting a class of economic phenomena, we hold that by nature it falls into this definition of discipline. At the present time, however, accounting cannot be regarded as a branch of systematized learning, mainly because it lacks a conceptual framework in a systematic sense to guide its explanations and predictions of accounting events.

The construction of a conceptual framework for an empirical discipline requires not only a set of formal rules (methodology) but also a clear understanding of the conditions of knowledge acquisition (epistemology). This book is intended to present a methodological exposition of theory construction and verification in accounting. It does not deal with accounting theory per se. Our main purpose is to explore the nature and function of theory as a well-structured form of knowledge that is true, logically and/or empirically. The word "structure" signifies the relationships among the building blocks of a theory.

For theory formation in empirical disciplines in general and in accounting in particular, we subscribe to the mode of thought known as logical empiricism, which, as contrasted with early empiricism, calls for equal emphasis on syntactical and semantical rules in theory formation. Our inclination toward the empirical mode of thought rests on the belief that all specific accounting assertions, once developed, must be subject to empirical validation

Because the social sciences deal with human behavior collectively or individually, they are often labeled value systems; accounting, although not a "science" yet, is not immune from value statements because it studies the socioeconomic activities of the human race. We wish to emphasize, however, that it is paramount in theory construction and verification to distinguish between positive and normative assertions, because "ought" statements do not, epistemologically speaking, necessarily entail "is" statements. Thus, we believe that it is methodologically necessary to differentiate between the positive and normative phases of accounting operations. As the discipline progresses, it is quite possible to have the two phases synthesized, but we believe that the former is necessarily the foundation of the latter. This is not to say that the fashionable goal-oriented deductive system is methodologically invalid. What is at issue is the verifiability of such a system without a positive frame of reference. The essence of the goal-determination issue is that it not only involves individuals' ideologies (value judgment with a future referent) but also imposes the formidable task of ranking a given society's value system, which is certainly beyond the accountant's domain. In brief, we maintain that the positive and normative phases of accounting are to be distinguished and that a synthesis of them may come only after a logically and empirically validated frame of reference has been established. In a practical sense, this also means that the analytical and reporting functions of accounting must be separated from its interpretative function.

Although each discipline is identified by the environment in which it functions, the classification

of disciplines is largely a matter of convenience
and necessity. The reason is twofold. First, all
segments of the total environment are interrelated.
Second, no single discipline of which we are aware
is large enough to cope with the total environment.
And yet, a common set of concepts is shared by all
disciplines, and each discipline deals only with
those properties of the concepts that are most
relevant to that discipline's orientation and function. To delineate a given discipline, one must,
in addition to acknowledging the relevant properties
of the common concepts, make certain assumptions.
When taken together, concepts and assumptions form
the foundation of the discipline in question.

Our exposition starts with a general discourse
on the meaning of systematized learning, theory,
and research methodology, which constitutes Chapter
2. Although systematized learning is defined in
terms of methods employed, it is maintained that
human knowledge, no matter how acquired, is always
fragmentary and that theories can never really
be complete (that is, they are always tentative
and subject to modification or replacement.) By
research methodology, we mean deduction, induction,
and a mixture of both. Induction characterizes
the very basic nature of empirical studies, but
deductive reasoning is a necessary part of the
scientific method. Without deduction, endless
observations and measurements would have to be made
in scientific inquiries, and this process would be
too costly and time-consuming. In addition, the
infiniteness of theoretical constructs can never

be fully explored by the inductive process. The
chapter also presents a general discussion of the
systems approach with particular reference to its
validity and limitations in research.

Chapter 3 presents an examination of the
various identities of the accounting discipline,
reflecting, in part, the diversified modes of
accounting thought existing at the present time.
The identity of accounting is a crucial issue
because it will, in large measure, determine the
orientation and function of the accounting discipline.
Chapter 4 provides a discussion of the fundamentals
of propositions (i.e., statements with truth values,
logical or empirical) and of concept formulation,
with particular emphasis on the distinction between
theoretical constructs and empirical concepts and
their relations. A critical examination of the
normative and positive modes of accounting thought
is presented in Chapter 5, with emphasis on their
epistemological foundations. Since accounting
depicts relevant events mostly in quantitative
terms, it is, we believe, of utmost importance
that we understand the meaning and function of
measurement and its relation to relevant constructs.
This problem is treated in Chapter 6. The remaining
three chapters are devoted to patterns of systematic
explanation. A general discussion of systematic
explanations is presented in Chapter 7, with
special reference to the foundation of a discipline,
formation, development and confirmation of
hypotheses, and conditions and methodological
requirements of accounting hypotheses. Chapter 8

offers a tentative set of accounting postulates,
not so much describing what accounting postulates
are but rather demonstrating the significance of
laying down the foundation upon which the discipline
is to be built and developed. Chapter 9 attempts,
in a methodological sense, to depict the essence
of the accounting model, particularly the interplay
of stocks and flows and the crucial relationships
between general and special hypotheses of accounting.

In summary, this book is intended to examine
the basic rules and principles that a researcher
must observe in conducting scientific inquiries,
together with the truth criteria which he must
follow in knowledge acquisition. It has been
contended that since accounting is not a scientific
discipline and since accounting "principles" are
man-made rules and do not reflect fundamental
truth, formal methodology and truth criteria are
inapplicable to accounting research. We reject
these contentions. In the first place, we believe
that all research should be conducted in an orderly,
consistent, and systematic manner. The most effective
way of accomplishing this is, so far as we know,
to follow the rules laid down by the logician, at
least until we can come up with a better alternative.
In the second place, we are not searching for the
fundamental or ultimate truth which is in the realm
of metaphysics. Since human knowledge is always
tentative and fragmentary, there is no guarantee of
the truth of our knowledge. We appeal, then, to
epistemology in general and to logical empiricism
in particular for the truth criteria of our knowledge.

In the third place, since accounting is, at present, in a transition period, evidenced by the extension of the accounting boundaries and interdisciplinary considerations in accounting research (most of which are in the domain of science—physical and social), we must be aware of the formal methodology and truth criteria employed in those other disciplines.

2 Systematized Learning and Research Methodology

In any attempt at theory construction, it is essential to have a firm grasp of the meaning of systematized learning which is often identified with scientific studies conducted under rigorous rules. The accounting discipline through the years has been, to say the least, deficient in structure and formal research methodology. A discourse on the structure of accounting theory, therefore, requires a good understanding initially of the meaning of systematized learning and its tools. The major purposes of this chapter are to present, in a general way, the nature of scientific inquiry and the significance of research methodology in theory formation.

The Meaning of Science

The term "science" has been interpreted in a

number of ways. For instance, science may be viewed as a field of study dealing with the knowns through scientific processes. Science may also be regarded as a field of analysis emphasizing generalizations of a given class or classes of phenomena. Still another interpretation is that science is the methods used in the process of studying the substance of a given area. Although these interpretations vary in breadth, and a demarcation between them is quite subtle, all of them stress the use of proper methodology in an inquiry. In general, we may say that methods define science.

Attempts at systemization of knowledge can be traced to ancient Egyptian and Babylonian observation of the periodicity of astronomic events. Some Ionian philosophers (including Pythagoras of Samos) used the observational method to study natural phenomena. The observational method of the Ionians for the study of metaphysics was discarded by later Greeks; Aristotle, however, did attempt biological experimentation. The Alexandrians, Aristarchus, and Hipparchus, in the third century B.C. used scientific methods in the study of astronomy. Not much progress was made on scientific methods until the thirteenth century, however, when Roger Bacon engaged in a fantastic work of compiling the scientific knowledge of his time. Since then, especially during the period of the Renaissance, the scope of scientific inquiry has been broadened. The scientific method as we know it today was formulated largely by philosophers of science in the last two centuries.

The ultimate goal of science is to formulate general *laws* which have the power to explain and to predict with a high degree of certainty. The process of scientific inquiry requires careful observation and measurement of the object in question. Careful observation is performed by a "trained" observer who is necessarily conditioned by his prior knowledge and experience. Measurement primarily involves quantification (assigning numerical value to objects observed), which calls not only for precise units of measure but, more importantly, for *operational* concepts. Critical analysis of what has been observed is imperative. This is generally followed by the process of synthesis. In the course of observation, the scientist is looking for similarities in the attributes of the object in question or the regularity of a class of phenomena. A scientific study requires a starting point, and the scientist must form hypotheses from which testable consequences are deduced.

It may be pointed out that the classification of science in terms of specialization is largely a matter of convenience. All sciences are interrelated, and because of this, new sciences are created from time to time (e.g., biochemistry). The distinction between the so-called "pure" and "applied" sciences relates to the level of inquiry proper and to the immediate application of scientifc laws. A crucial issue in science classification is the distinction between the natural sciences and the social sciences. To many "purists," the latter are often regarded as

"pseudo sciences"; however, this is not necessarily
a discomforting note. In the first place, the social
sciences, *qua* science, are relatively young. In the
second place, phenomena and variables in the general
area of the social sciences are often too complicated
and numerous for the social scientist to comprehend,
control, and experiment with, especially in light of
existing scientific methods and techniques. As long
as an inquiry employs scientific methodology and
attempts to systemize a body of knowledge, however,
that inquiry is in the domain of science.

Hypotheses, Theories, Models, and Laws

There are a number of terms, such as "hypotheses,"
"theories," "models," and "laws," which are of
particular importance to theorization. Some of these
terms connote essentially the same meaning and can
be used interchangeably. Others vary in degree of
exactness or certainty; hence they must be properly
differentiated. Precise and explicit identification
of these terms in a scientific inquiry is necessary,
because ambiguous terms used indiscriminately lead
to confusion.

Theory is, in general, expressed in a set of
propositions which are logically consistent and
some of which have been tested, verified, or
confirmed. It should be stated that no theory
derived from human experience can be unassailably
proved or certain. A particular theory is accepted
as valid or true in the absence of a better theory.
In addition, there are often competing theories
in a given field. The lack of complete certainty

in a given theory signifies that human knowledge is always *probable*. The delicate situation in knowledge acquisition is that even "obvious facts" may not be facts or truths, not to mention "relations" of facts. The most one can say about theories is that they provide us with a degree of confidence or assurance in explaining and, possibly, predicting a certain class of phenomena of the existential world. Complete verification of a theory is unattainable, and it is in this sense that a theory can never be said to be completely finished or confirmed. Thus, a theory is constantly being tested, revised, improved, or replaced by a better one.

The distinction between "theory" and "hypothesis" is primarily a matter of degree of formalization. In general, we may say that a hypothesis is a tentative explanation of a given problem or situation. It is often used by the theorist as a working basis for subsequent operations and may be regarded as a conjecture to guide an argument or to lead to theory formation. Thus, as compared with theories, hypotheses are less formal and certain. Hypotheses may be formulated either deductively or inductively. When a hypothesis has been satisfactorily developed, tested, and verified, it may become a theory. An existing theory is the one which provides the best kind of explanation and prediction that we have constructed for the time being and which awaits emergence of a better one. Thus, strictly speaking, no theory is absolutely certain and satisfactory. Because of this, some scientists use the terms "theory" and

"hypothesis" interchangeably. In this book, however,
we shall try to differentiate between these terms
whenever possible.

Theory construction often involves model building
—an invaluable tool in scientific study. This is so
either because of the complexity of reality or because
of the scientist's preference for simplicity for
the sake of subsequent manipulation. Thus, a model
is essentially a simplified picture, imitation,
image, or analogy of reality. In general, it is a
structure composed of organized and interrelated
elements. The major advantages of models are their
simplicity and logical clarity. But these may become
the fundamental dangers of models when simplicity
becomes oversimplicity and when logical clarity is
made at the expense of distorting reality. When
extended, models may become theories. The distinction
between models and theories is sometimes a matter of
elaboration and the degree of verification, and it is
in this sense that some theorists regard them as
synonymous terms. The term "law," as compared to
"theory," connotes a greater degree of exactness or
certainty. As such, its use is more appropriate
in the physical sciences than in the social sciences.

Structure and System

Logic is the study of "forms", which have no
factual contents. A logical form shows how a thing
is constructed or how its constituents are put
together. Such a form is known as a "structure". The
constituents of a structure may be physical or non-
physical and are so arranged or constructed as to

reflect their relationships. A theory structure is
the form in which its elements or parts are organized
in an orderly fashion so as to signify their internal
relationships.

A system is a systematic and comprehensive
assemblage of things or parts forming a complex or
unitary whole. The term itself connotes a scheme
of classification and may refer to any orderly
arrangement of facts, principles, rules, or methods
in a given field. For instance, "deductive *system*,"
"inductive *system*," and "mixed *system*" are good
examples of the term's usage.

The distinction between a structure and a
system is sometimes flimsy and, to some extent,
they overlap. Upon closer examination, however, we
see that "structure" refers to the connections among
the elements of an object or among their constituent
relations, and that it is more concerned with how
the object is constructed. Thus, the term "structure"
may be used to denote the construct of a proposition
or the way in which the elements of the proposition
are logically put together. A system is more akin to
an orderly classification and organization of, say,
several sets of propositions; a system takes a higher
form of structure—meaning that it arranges or assembles
units or parts into a whole body of systematized
knowledge. A structure reflects the relationships of
parts or elements, while a system sets forth the
boundaries of a given "whole." For instance, "the
structure of industries" refers to the interrelationships of the various industries which are the parts

or components of an economy. On the other hand,
when we speak of an economic *system*, we are referring
to the boundaries or range within which a given
economic system as a whole is classified.

Research Methodology

Methodology is a general term referring to a
system of methods, principles, rules, and procedures
underlying the conduct of inquiry. By research
methodology, we mean formal methodology which
includes deduction, induction, and mixed systems.
Methodology itself is a field of study; therefore,
only general statements can be made here about
this subject.

Deduction — A deductive system starts with a set
of basic propositions about the subject under
study. Some of these propositions are derived from
certain facts which must be known ab initio. These
facts are supposed to be so simple that they can be
known immediately, that is, they are self-evident,
indubitable truths. Under the classical example of
Euclid's geometry, these self-evident statements
are known as "axioms".Other initial propositions
are a set of assumed statements which must be
taken for granted. They are known as "postulates".
The distinction between axioms and postulates is
not always sharp, and, as a matter of fact, Euclid
himself did not always make a clear differentiation
between these two types of statements. For our
purposes here, we shall use the general term
"postulates" for all initial propositions under a
deductive system.

A postulate possesses a number of characteristics which may be regarded as tests to be applied to any proposition as a basic statement under a deductive system. To be a postulate, it must meet the following requirements: (1) coherence — it shall belong to the system and must cohere with the rest; (2) contributiveness — it shall imply further propositions of the system, (3) consistency — it shall not contradict any other postulate of the system; (4) independence — it shall not itself be implied by other postulates of the system; if not, it is a theorem, not a postulate.[1] A postulate can be implied only by itself. We may prove a theorem but not a postulate.

Although a system of deductive logic begins with a set of "unproved" primitive propositions, one wonders how such a set is first derived or selected in areas other than pure mathematics and logic. The answer is that the selection of a set of primitive propositions must fall outside the system. At this stage of theorization, the theorist must be most careful in selecting and forming his postulates. As will be discussed in Chapter 4, "self-evidence" often turns out to be a very questionable notion and "known by intuition" may be quite deceptive. Under a deductive system, however, once a set of postulates is accepted as valid, it must be treated as a priori. The next step, using the logical rules of inference, is to deduce other propositions from the postulates. A set of exact definitions is indispensable for guiding operations. The deduced propositions in their form are known as theorems.

Under deduction, the validity of theorems depends
entirely upon the initial set of propositions. As
long as the theorems correspond to, or are logically
consistent with the given set of postulates, they
are valid conclusions. This means that it is
entirely possible to formulate different sets of
theorems under different sets of postulates for a
given area of study. Incompatible theorems under a
given deductive system occur only when inconsistent
postulates are included in the system. It may be
noted that a deductive system is a *closed* system,
and that empirical verification of the deduced
theorems is not a part of the system. It is in this
sense that deductively derived conclusions contain
the elements of certainty and timelessness. Except
in mathematics and logic, purely deductive logic
(i.e., deductive logic proper) is rarely employed in
scientific inquiries. Following a deductive system
means, in most cases, to carry out the procedures
of deductive logic, often implemented by other
systems.

Induction — The system of inductive logic consists
of both observations and measurements from which
generalized statements are drawn. An inductive
process often begins with observation of a number
of instances. The essence of the observation
process is to look for "likes" or "similarities"
of these instances. Observed events call for
proper measurement. In an inductive system, truth
values must be separately assigned to each proposition by outside information or by pure assumption;

in the latter case, empirical verification is necessary.
In other words, unlike deduction, the truth or falsity
of a proposition under an inductive system is not
implied by other propositions. The basic theme of
induction is that observation of sufficient instances
will give us a degree of assurance, so as to generalize
the entire universe or a class of similar phenomena.
Although premises or hypotheses may be proposed under
an inductive system, there is no such requirement as
logical correspondence between the premises and
conclusions. The premises could be true, but the
conclusion false; or the conclusion could have a truth
value independent of the premises. Thus, an inductively
derived conclusion requires outside support.

Generalizations resulting from an inductive
process are always *probable*. It is always risky to
use the word *all*, if we know only *some*. Consequently,
induction always contains an element of falsity,
and we necessarily bear the so-called inductive
risk.   There is no doubt that the scientist
assigns probablities to inductively derived conclusions. "Perfect" induction is humanly unattainable.
Although induction does not possess the kind of
logical elegance and certainty that deduction enjoys,
the strength of induction lies in the fact that we
have succeeded in this risky business. One may
speculate that without inductive reasoning the
human race would have been wiped out a long time
ago. Since we cannot learn from the future, we must
rely upon past and present instances to anticipate
future experience. It is in this sense that

induction seems also to go beyond the present time
limit, restrained by varying degrees of probability.

Although the inductive method was first described
by Aristotle (who, however, was concerned mainly
with the deductive method), systematic development
of the inductive method was made largely by Francis
Bacon in the seventeenth century, the English
empiricists (particularly David Hume) in the eighteenth
century, and John Stuart Mill in the nineteenth
century. In advocating and developing the inductive
method, these philosophers postulated a law of "the
uniformity of nature." In doing so, they presumed
a correspondence of cause and effect in identical
or similar circumstances. Under induction, however,
such a "causality" has not been accepted by modern
empiricists. For one thing, it is not possible to
identify the totality of conditions surrounding an
experiment. For another, it is not always possible
to reproduce identical conditions for subsequent
experiments. What happened once does not necessarily
guarantee that the same thing will happen again.
Thus, the "if A then B" reasoning does not always
prevail in inductive logic. In inductive reasoning,
we need continuous assurance.

Deduction, Induction and the Scientific Method —
Although the "form" of deductive logic starts with
a set of unproved, primitive propositions, the
formulation of such a set of propositions—except
in the areas of pure mathematics and logic—is
often made by inductive reasoning and is necessarily
conditioned by the theorist's previous knowledge

and experience. It is in this sense that we may say
inductive logic presupposes deductive logic. One
must realize that the certainty and exactness of the
conclusions from a deductive process are no more than
analysis of the meanings and relations of the words
contained in the given set of postulates. The main
problematic area of deduction lies in the formation
of a set of initial propositions from information
outside the system. This means that the truth
values of these propostions are *probable* in the
first place. Deductively derived conclusions are
valid, certain, or indubitable only in a logical
sense. In case we doubt our conclusions under a
deductive system, the only channel we have for
substantiating them is from within the system, that is,
to trace back to the original premises. Empirical
confirmation, verification, or modification of
deductively derived statements necessitates the use
of inductive processes.

It would be a mistake to feel that, because
of the level of logical rigorousness and certainty,
induction is inferior to deduction. We cannot
know merely by a critical exercise of the mind.
Knowledge is acquired through a process of interaction of the mind and the outside world. If we
do not rely on our perception, prior experience,
or the tested methods of induction, "We may not
survive long enough to enjoy the certainty of
deduction."[2] It is interesting to note that the
momentum of science greatly increased after the
systematic development of induction in the

seventeenth century. On the other hand, observation
does not mean observing in a random manner. The mere
decision as to what to observe reflects the observer's
preconceived notions, which not only set forth the
initial position that he takes but which are conditioned
by his prior knowledge and experience as well. Such a
position is necessarily a priori. Thus, inductive
reasoning requires, explicitly or implicitly, some
premises with which to start. Further, theory
construction requires the use of both syntactical
and semantical rules. Moreover, theorization may
call for those propositions which are not capable
of being verified empirically. In addition, in
terms of economy, extension, explication of hypotheses,
and formulation of highly advanced constructs,
deductive logic is extremely powerful.

From the above discussion, it is clear that one
rarely finds a scientific system which is either purely
deductive or entirely inductive. Most systems are of
a hybrid nature, that is, they are partially formed and
developed under deductive reasoning but also contain
a large number of facts which could never have been
inferred. In addition, some propositions may have no
empirical correspondence but are needed for facilitating
the formulation of a theory. On the other hand,
complete verification of a generalized statement is
not attainable.

The unfortunate conflict between deduction and
induction long has been a heated issue among
philosophers. A historical contrast between these
types of reasoning would reveal the traditional feud

between rationalists and empiricists — the former
advocate that we can know by *reason* only, while the
latter emphasize knowledge acquisition through
experience and empirical correspondence. In the
classical case of "the motion of the heart and the
blood," involving René Descartes, a master of
mathematical method, and William Harvey, a master of
experimental technique, it turns out that neither
one used deduction (Descartes) or induction (Harvey)
exclusively; it was a matter of emphasis.[3] In
knowledge acquisition, we need *support* as well as
reason. The dream of every scientist, of course, is
to arrange his data in a formal structure with complete
certainty and exactness, but such a dream will
probably remain a dream.

The scientist almost always talks about the use
of "scientific method" in his work. Just what is
meant by "scientific method" is not always clear
and precise. As a matter of fact, the substance
of scientific method varies from one scientist to
another. In general, it is a process of inquiry
requiring the use of both deduction and induction
with emphasis placed on the latter (and experimentation), treating the former as a part of the whole
system. Diagrams *2-1* and *2-1a* depict, in a general
way, the scheme of the scientific method.

A scientific study often begins with observation
of a class of phenomena. Both analysis and synthesis
are performed in the process. The ultimate goal is
to formulate general laws or, to a lesser degree,
theories or principles. The working basis for

Diagram 2-1
The Scientific Method

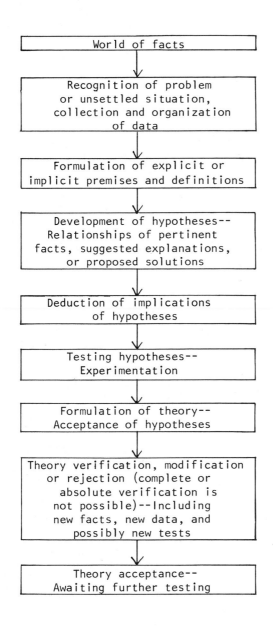

Diagram 2-1a

The Scientific Method

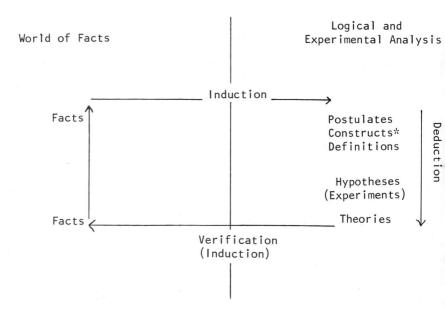

* See the section dealing with "Concept Formulation" presented in Chapter 4.

657.01   Y9a
c.1

subsequent operations is the derivation of a hypothesis.
One may posit a hypothesis by using the so-called
hypothetical-deductive method, which means that a
theory is only a hypothesis assumed for the time
being. Testable consequences are then deduced from
the hypothesis awaiting disproof. When disproved,
the hypothesis is replaced by a new posit. When
proved, the hypothesis is elevated to the status
of a theory. For a given field of study, different
scientists with different working bases (hypotheses)
may devise different theories. The ideal situation
is to consolidate all the theories into a *general*
theory. Thus, a healthy symptom in any field is the
existence of competing and complementary theories.

The use of the scientific method initially
calls for identification or recognition of a problem
or unsettled situation. The urge to pursue the
problem or unsettled situation may be due to
intellectual curiosity or the existence of a crisis.
In any event, the immediate action is to collect and
organize relevant data so as to illuminate the problem
in question, with emphasis placed on exploring the
relations of the facts or phenomena relevant to the
situation. Methodologically speaking, facts by
themselves are meaningless. But when they are
received by a person who is familiar with the basic
concepts of a given discipline, they will be so treated
and synthesized as to provide a basis for further
study. This is followed by positing a tentative
solution. A hypothesis is not merely a postulated
statement without any factual content. It may take

the form of a tentative generalization based upon preliminary observation or may be largely conjectural in nature. The derivation of a hypothesis may also require a set of postulates and definitions as its working frame. Testable consequences then are deduced from the hypothesis for subsequent operations. The hypothesis must be proved or disproved through reasoning (including logical and mathematical manipulations) and experimentation. Ideally, the experimentation must be so designed and controlled as to be reproducible. If the results of a series of experiment agree with the hypothesis, the validity of the hypothes is elevated. In the area of the social sciences, controlled experimentatioh is rarely attainable. We must, therefore, conduct our "experimentation" through extensive empirical verification. Absolute verification (confirmation or refutation) is not possible, for it will require an infinite number of operations. The final acceptance of a tested hypothesis is necessarily a matter of degree of confidence. The scientist thinks in terms of probabilism, not in terms of absolute truth. In the process of verification or experimentation, new facts and new data may provide additional information and may call for modification or even rejection of the original hypothesis, followed either by the formation of a new hypothesis or by the conducting of additional experiments. When the tentative solution is finally accepted as theory, the process ends only for the time being, since theories are never really finished. The whole process of scientific inquiry is a continuous one and involves a back-and-forth movement. The process should not be viewed as a vicious cycle, however, because a better understanding of the problem at issue usually is acquired after each round.

The Systems Approach and General Systems Theory
―― In recent years, the systems approach has found a wide range of followers in a number of disciplines. It is an approach which is opposite to the traditional analytic or mechanistic approach. Under the mechanistic approach, the whole is studied by analyzing its parts which determine the characteristics of the whole. Under the systems approach, it is the whole which determines the characteristics of the parts. The differences between these two approaches do not end here, however, because supporters of the systems approach would argue further that the traditional mechanistic approach fails to account for the order and inter-relatedness of the parts of a whole. In addition, the purpose of a given entity is determined by the whole, not by its parts, because parts alone have no purposes. Moreover, as it goes, there are *new* properties which *emerge* when the parts of a whole enter into relationships with one another.

It has been said that many disciplines have followed a macro-micro (systems-mechanistic) cycle.[4] For instance, in physics, the cycle moves from Newton's universal viewpoint to the analytical pattern of classical physics, and to the macro approach of modern physics; in economics, from

Adam Smith's *Wealth of Nations* to the theory of the firm, and to John Maynard Keynes' general theory; and, in organizational theory, from the classic school's macro approach to the neoclassical school's micro approach, and back to a macro approach under modern organization theory.

The systems approach is indeed appealing and there is no denial of its value to certain scientific inquiries. The approach, however, particularly in light of the general systems theory, has been a controversial issue among philosophers and scientists; therefore, we should be aware of its inherent problems and limitations in application. To begin with, let us examine briefly its philosophical foundation.

The Philosophical Foundations of General Systems Theory and the Problem of Emergence. By and large, the basic idea of system study came from the German philosopher Georg Hegel. Hegel's writings are among the most difficult to read. If we understand correctly knowledge, for Hegel, can be set forth only in the form of system, and truth can be realized only by systematic development. His reasoning goes as follows: one starts with a certain position called the *thesis*, which within itself contains the seeds of its destruction or negation; the negation eventually becomes the *antithesis*. The opposition between thesis and antithesis promotes thought to a higher level, containing elements of both, called the *synthesis*. What characterizes thought also characterizes reality. Reality cannot be studied

successfully by dividing it into parts. When a part
is isolated, it is no longer a part of the whole, so
its nature changes. Thus in view of wholeness,
parts are organically or internally interrelated,
and the parts are affected and altered by their
interrelationships. This theory of internal
relations was made clear by the Oxford Hegelian
philosopher F. H. Bradley. He contends that when
entity A of a system enters into a relationship
with entity B of the system, it gains a new property
P resulting from this relationship. Without the
relationship, A would be different, and, as a matter
of fact, it would not be A.[5]

The Hegelian thesis of internal relations has
been seriously attacked through the years. One such
attack is based on the distinction between the
defining and *accompanying* characteristics of an
entity. The former define the term used for the
entity, while the presence or absence of the latter
has no effect on the use of the term, that is,
accompanying characteristics are not defining.[6]
G. E. Moore contends that the relations with other
entities into which A enters are not necessarily
defining characteristics. It is possible, thus,
for A to enter into a relationship but still remain
unchanged.[7]

The theory of internal relations is intimately
related to the philosophical problem "emergence,"
the essence of which may be illustrated by the
combination of the atoms of hydrogen and oxygen
which emerges with an unpredictable result— water

(H_2O). The message from the general systems theorist is that the failure of the traditional mechanistic approach to account for the whole provides incomplete explanations of reality. Although it is not possible to deduce water either from hydrogen or oxygen alone, Ernest Nagel argues that it is not properties, but propositions which can be deduced; and unless something has already been said in the premises, nothing can be deduced from them.[8] Nagel further argues that variants of theory about the same subject matter postulate variously its constituents and characteristics. Thus, although a property may indeed be an emerging trail under one variant of the theory, it need not be so under other variants.[9]

The Meaning of Wholeness and Unity of Knowledge.
A controversial feature of the systems theory is the contention that every part is related to everything else and each given "system" is merely a subsystem of something larger. If we follow this line of reasoning, it will eventually lead to the quest of *whole* knowledge which is humanly impossible. In addition, the word "whole" has been defined in a variety of ways, and its meaning is not always clear unless one of its meanings is defined in the context of a specific application. Furthermore, it is sometimes confused with the word "sum." Nagel[10] distinguishes the meaning of the whole in eight different senses, of which he relates the last one to the systems theory as follows:

> Finally, the word "whole" is often used
> to refer to any system whose spatial parts
> stand to each other in various relations

of dynamical dependence. Many of the so-called "organic unities" appear to be systems of this type.

Biologists are among the strongest supporters of the systems approach and theory. This is understandable because organisms are probably among the most complicated systems. For instance, instead of studying soil and plant as separate elements, it would be more meaningful to study them together as a complex whole because of their inter-action. A leading proponent of this view is Ludwig von Bertalanffy who contends that general systems theory with emphasis on the complex whole-ness of elements provides *general* principles holding for any systems.[11] Thus, a basic goal of general systems theory is to unify sciences and to formulate "a body of systematic theoretical constructs which will discuss the general relationships of the empirical world."[12] In other words, it aims at a unity of knowledge in terms of a system of systems. The theme is synthesis, and the faith lies in the belief that there are common constructs shared by all sciences. As such, general systems theory is very much interdisciplinary in nature.

Nonadditiveness of Functional Wholes. One of the debatable issues with respect to the whole and its parts is the contention that an organic or "functional" whole is nonadditive. That is, the behavior of the whole is not determined by that of its individual elements. The expression "the whole is more than the sum of its parts" takes the same point of view. Nagel goes into some

lengthy discussion to refute the sharp distinction
between functional wholes and "nonfunctional"
("summative") wholes in terms of additivity or
nonadditivity, because parts of summative wholes
also stand in relations of causal interdependence.[13]
To Nagel, whether an analysis is additive or
nonadditive depends largely upon its specific
assumptions and the application of specific theory
to the analysis in the light of specified purposes,
from which deduction is performed (i.e., nothing
can be deduced from assumptions devoid of such
implications—a *logical* fact).[14]

Systems Operationally Defined.   Short of the
ultimate whole or system (the universe as a whole or
something larger perhaps), we need an operational
definition of system.   Definitions of system
given by general systems theorists are often too
general.   For instance, Bertalanffy defines a
system as a "complex of elements in mutual
interactions;"[15] Anatol Rapaport says that a "whole
which functions as a whole by virtue of the interdependence of its parts is called a system;"[16]
and R. L. Ackoff regards a system as any enity
which consists of independent parts.[17]   All of
these definitions are quite similar, but they tell
us very little about the boundaries of a system.
One alternative is to select a group of interrelated
elements relevant to a given inquiry and call it
a system.[18]   This approach, however, would require
the researcher to identify the individual relevant
elements and *sever* them from other elements *before*

a system could be formed. It would not only violate
the basic idea of the systems theory but would
also call for the use of the traditional mechanistic
method at the beginning in order to deal with the
separate elements. As chided by D. C. Phillips,
"...He is doing the very thing that his own creed
tells him should not be done."[19]

Even though we have no answer to the conceptual
magnitude of systems under the systems theory,
there is a practical way of getting out of this
dilemma. We know that the degree of abstraction
or generality of study under general systems theory
progresses as one moves from one level of study to
the next one. Accordingly, we can avoid the fatal
blow of ultimate generality if we stay at low
levels of systems analysis. It is exactly in
this manner that the use of the systems approach in
information theory, game theory, factor analysis,
and so forth has been quite operational. In other
words, instead of dealing with system in an infinite
sense, we stop at a *partial* or subsystem level and
accept subsystems as systems in their own right.
It may be noted that, regressively, subsystems
are composed of parts, which are also subsystems
of an infinite order. Where then is the stopping
point? For individual disciplines, "systems" may
be defined as their respective units of study,
for example, the organism of biology, the organization
of organization theory, the economy of macroeconomics,
the firm of microeconomics, and the accounting entity
of accounting. This definition of system is a

matter not only of expediency but is also a necessity, if we wish to put the systems approach to practical use.

Relevance of the Systems Approach to Accounting Research. With an awareness of the inherent problems and limitations of the systems approach and general systems theory, as expounded above, we believe that the systems approach (in a *partial* sense, of course) can be quite relevant and effective with respect to the following phases of theory formation in accounting:[20]

   a) It will enable us to identify more effectively the unit of study in accounting— the accounting *system*.

   b) It will make us aware of the importance of interdisciplinary considerations.

   c) It will recognize all the subsystems and, most of all, their interrelationships in light of the general accounting system. In addition, it will enable us to detect gaps among the subsystems and any isolated subsystems.

   d) In light of the general system, it will direct our attention to any missing components that are crucial to the accounting system. For instance, gaps between some subsystems may indicate the need of additional subsystems.

   e) It will help us develop a "spectrum" of accounting theories, particularly in

terms of degree of abstraction and
generality.

(f) As will be discussed in Chapter 9, the
     systems approach and general systems
     theory will be most effective in
     formulating and synthesizing submodels
     of accounting.

(g) In general, it *implements* the analytic
     approach.

Logic and Science

Logical forms are highly abstract. The
elegance and power of logic lies in the degree
of abstraction, that is, from concrete to abstract,
from forms with contents to those forms without
contents, and from instances to concepts. Logic
is an indispensable tool in any scientific study.
Science goes beyond mere logical rigor, however,
for science is not without factual contents. If
we were to study only the logical implications of
propositions, then logic would be the only *science*.
Science seeks explanations of the behaviors and
relations of a certain class of phenomena and
provides a basis for anticipating future phenomena
or experience. In order to anticipate the future,
we must know a great deal of the past and the
present, since we cannot learn from the future
which does not yet exist. To know is much more
than to acquire facts. We must abstract and
generalize from facts with past experience as our
reference point. Abstracting from reality, guarding
against inconsistency, and drawing out the

implications of a set of propositions necessitate
an exercise of rigorous logic. Without a logical
structure, our study would become an unsystematic
way of learning. Besides its highly abstract section,
however, the validity of a scientific study also
rests upon its empirical correspondence, without
which the study would be meaningless or irrelevant
to our beliefs about the existential world. Thus,
purely deduced statements from a priori propositions
provide *logical* truths only. In the final analysis,
we may say that although logic is indispensable in
any scientific inquiry, so far as end results are
concerned, it plays only a secondary role. In other
words, it is merely a tool. A word of warning to
the beginning student of science is in order: except
in mathematics and logic, purely deductive systems
provide us with no *new* knowledge; deduction is, at
most, only an intermediate process of the whole
scientific method. We recognize that the temptation
to pursue the logical elegance of deduction is
always strong, but in scientific studies, especially
those in the area of accounting, we must guard
ourselves from falling into the trap of the so-called
 axiomatic system, which employs, among other
things, a set of self-evident or indubitable
propositions.

Theories, Facts, and Practices

   It is said that deduction is a process of
reasoning which takes us from the general to the
particular. Verification is not an integral part
of deductive logic. Inferences from a set of

premises, which is accepted as a priori under
deduction, however, actually add nothing new to our
knowledge except in a psychological sense; that is,
we have not realized what we already know or, at
least, what we are supposed to know, from the
premises. Induction, on the other hand, takes
us from the particular to the general. The factual
content of inductively inferred beliefs is quite
immediate and direct in the early stage of theory
formation, where we use mostly observational terms.
As the process of generalization advances, more
and more abstract (theoretical) terms are employed,
and the generalized statements become increasingly
general, broad, and abstract. Thus, the back-and-
forth movement between facts and abstractions may
seem to have lost its trace in the "final" generalized
statements. This "gap" between facts and theories
is unavoidable because of abstraction, and the
magnitude of the gap depends partly upon the degree
of abstraction and partly upon the content of the
particulars observed and synthesized. But we
should never lose sight of the fact that a theory
or a generalized proposition is subject to subsequent
tests. In addition, experiments used to test the
implications (deduced), either of the original or
of the refined hypothesis, are conducted under
controlled conditions which are supposed to be
reproducible. Practical constraints undoubtedly
will limit the extent or range of the applicability
of a theory. An application of a given theory
means, roughly speaking, a movement from the general
to the particulars. A theory may be formulated

ahead of immediate application or current practices.
When this occurs, there is no gap involved, since
the theory corresponds to a mode of operation that
is not currently being engaged.

Although theory verification, when needed, is
always partial in the sense that we can observe
only particulars, confirmation or refutation of a
theory can be made only on a general scale. One
or a few instances do not confirm or refute a
theory. Facts alone are meaningless, unless their
relationships are explicated and interpreted in
light of a relevant theory. In addition, facts
are particulars and reflect a limited number of
individual events, while a theory is general and
broad and covers an unlimited number of phenomena
of the same class.

Because facts are expressed in observational
terms and theories are stated in abstract terms,
we need the rules of interpretation to reconcile
the gap between theories and facts and between
theories and practices. In addition, a theoretical
framework is followed not only to guide practical
operations but also to evalute soundness of
practices.

Scientific studies require the use of the
so-called operational concepts. Under the
doctrine of operationalism, each scientific concept
must be related to experience in terms of being
operationally defined so that it can be tested
and applied in subsequent operations. Operationalism
may be viewed as a modern version of empiricism.
The latter is a philosophical school of thought

which, in its many variants, holds that knowledge
acquisition originates in sense experience and
that only verifiable propositions are meaningful.
Although empiricism is undoubtedly the most
popular tenet of modern philosophy, we need to
clarify a crucial point here: Not every theoretical
concept is operationally definable and testable.
Further discussion of operational concepts is
presented in Chapter 4.

The Social Sciences vs. the Physical Sciences
    The scientific method is an integrated part
of the domain of science. The issue which concerns
us most here is whether the successful application
of the scientific method to the physical sciences
can be extended to the social sciences. This
statement poses an immediate question to which we
have no clear-cut answer: Are the social sciences,
qua science, sciences at all? To the hardcore
physical scientist, the social sciences are really
value systems, and hence they are arts not sciences.
The "value" issue will be discussed in Chapter 5.
It is sufficient here, however, to say that value
judgment is unavoidable in all scientific inquiries
(e.g., goal determination, the direction of a
research endeavor, or the manner in which an inquiry
is conducted, all of which require some kind of
value judgment). The question apparently is of
the degree of relying on value statements in a
scientific inquiry. Further, value judgment, when
limited to the minimum extent, does not necessarily
impair the objectivity of a discipline or its

scientific nature. Moreover, interpretation and
application of the results of a scientific study
must be distinguished from the scientific study
itself.

The complex nature of the social sciences
may be illuminated by a general comparison with
the nature of the physical sciences. First, the
major subject under study in the area of the social
sciences is the human being which, in terms of
motivation, behavior, and relations, is probably
the most complicated and unpredictable creature
known. On the other hand, the objects dealt with
by the physical scientist are, in general, orderly
and predictable, save for the complication contributed by the scientist's emotive overtones or
value judgments. Second, physical events are,
relatively speaking, simpler to observe and to
generalize, because of their repetitive nature or
regularity, than are social phenomena, which are
either generally nonrepetitive or are lacking in
regularity or orderly frequency. Third, for the
purposes of observation and generalization, it is
quite difficult to isolate a class of social
phenomena from the *total* cultural environment.
The interrelatedness of the various aspects of the
socioeconomic environment can hardly be overstated.
There are just too many outside forces or variables
which are either out of control or unpredictable
for experimental purposes. Fourth, the lack of
controlled experiments in the area of the social
sciences is undoubtedly a major handicap in
utilizing the scientific method. In addition,

data collected for research purposes in the social
sciences are usually not only incomplete but, more
important, are not the design of the social
scientist. The physical scientist has the
advantages of conducting controlled experiments,
creating and designing his own data, and reproducing
identical experiments. Fifth, many socioeconomic
phenomena are not capable of being directly
observed or measured. The measurement theory
which is well developed in the physical sciences
is, at most, in its infant stage in the social
sciences. For one thing, mathematics has not yet
advanced to the extent that it can serve as an
adequate tool for the social scientist. For
another, verification, as well as prediction, is
much more difficult to carry out in the social
sciences, because of lack of effective yardsticks
for precise measurement, the need for a longer
period for verification or confirmation of predicted
statements, and the ever changing conditions of the
human world. Finally, while emotive bias is
unavoidable in all human endeavors, the social
scientist, as compared with the physical scientist,
is in a much more disadvantageous position, since
the social scientist himself is part of the
general object being studied.

The preceding comparison probably sounds
quite disappointing to the social scientist. We
may take momentary comfort, however, from the fact
that the history of science shows that each
scientific discipline appears to be going nowhere
in the beginning. In addition, a young science

almost always starts with the formation of *simple* theories, which are later extended to cover a wider range of instances. This point is of particular relevance to the social sciences in light of the complexity of the social phenomena. The social scientist should be on guard with respect to emotive connotations or judgments, however, particularly in the stage of theory formulation (theory interpretation is a subsequent operation). The temptation to arrive at "desirable results" in light of socioeconomic goals is indeed too strong for the social scientist to maintain a state of scientific thinking. Another difficulty the social scientist encounters in doing scientific work is that of the use of "everyday" language, which is often vague and ambiguous. The social scientist should not only design precise terms but should also, whenever possible, have them symbolized.

In view of the numerous difficulties, the social sciences clearly have a long way to go to attain the kind of scientific elegance now enjoyed by the physical sciences. Most philosophers of science would agree, however, that so far as research methodology is concerned, there are no essential differences between the social sciences and the physical sciences, since research methodology represents merely systematic ways of conducting inquiries.

[1]Susanne K. Langer, An Introduction to Symbolic Logic. (New York: Dover Publications, Inc., 1957), pp. 185-6.

[2]Neal W. Klausner and Paul G. Kuntz, *Philosophy: The Study of Alternative Beliefs* (New York: The Macmillan Company, 1961), p. 144.

[3]René Descartes, *Discourse on Method*, trans. Laurence J. Lafleur, (New York: The Liberal Arts Press, 1950), pp. 30-32; Harvey, William, *Motion of the Heart and Blood* (Chicago: Henry Regnery Co., 1949).

[4]William G. Scott, *Human Relations in Management*. (Richard D. Irwin, Inc., 1962), pp. 152-54.

[5]F. H. Bradley, *Appearance and Reality* (Oxford University Press, 1962), pp. 513-19.

[6]John Hoopers, *An Introduction to Philosophical Analysis*, rev. ed. (Routledge and Kegan Paul, 1967), Chap. 1.

[7]D. C. Phillips, "Systems Theory -- A Discredited Philosophy." *Abacus*, (1969):6.

[8]Ernest Nagel, *The Structure of Science* (Harcourt, Brace & World, Inc., 1961), pp. 368-69.

[9]Ibid., pp. 369-71.

[10]Ibid., p. 383.

[11]Ludwig von Bertalanffy, Problem of Life (New York: Harper and Brothers, 1960) p. 199; see also his Modern Theories of Development, J. W. Woodger trans. (New York: Harper Torchbooks, 1962).

[12]Kenneth E. Boulding, "General Systems Theory: The Skeleton of Science." Management of Science, (1956):156.

[13]Nagel, op. cit., pp. 391-96.

[14]Ibid.

[15]Bertalanffy, op. cit., p. 11.

[16]Walter Buckley, ed., *Modern Systems Research for the Behavioral Scientist.* (Chicago: University of Chicago Press, 1968), p. xvii.

[17]R. L. Ackoff, "Systems, Organizations, and Interdisciplinary Research," *Systems, Research and Design,* ed. Donald P. Eckman (New York: John Wiley & Sons, Inc., 1961), pp. 27-8.

[18]A. D. Hall and Ragen, "Definition of System," Buckley, op. cit.

[19]Phillips, op. cit., p. 11.

[20](Some of the points have been expounded by) Charles H. Smith, (in his) "The Modern Systems Approach, General System Theory, and Accounting Development in the Age of Synthesis," The International Journal of Accounting, Spring, 1971, pp. 65-71.

3 The Accounting Discipline and Its Boundaries

The Various Versions of the Accounting Discipline

In one sense, a discipline may mean a body of specified instructions and exercises designed to train to proper conduct, behavior, or action; or it may mean a set of established rules and regulations guiding or controlling action or performance. Alternatively, a discipline may be viewed as a branch of learning requiring the use of proper methodology. Conventional accounting is a discipline in the former sense. In general, it contains a body of rules, which are conditioned largely by daily practices and supported by authoritative "opinions" or pronouncements. A discipline which is based on authoritative supports and daily practices "contains the 'lowest' level of theory, and this type of discipline can never be classified as a 'science.'"[1] It is exactly in this sense that conventional accounting

is defined as a practical art. A practical art
denotes any craft requiring the use of skills and
techniques acquired mostly from experience in an
unsystematic manner. This is simply another way
of saying that conventional accounting is "what
the accountant practices." When accounting is so
defined, it foregoes any possibility of acquiring
a *formal* structure. Thus, conventional accounting
has no methodological foundation, and therefore
it will receive no emphasis in this syllabus.

In recent years, conscientious efforts have
been made to broaden the scope of accounting and
to treat it as an effective vehicle for providing
meaningful information, particularly in a systematized sense. The movement of changing accounting
from the status of a practical art to something
else is still in motion, and the end is not yet in
sight. A very noticeable symptom of accounting
today is that it suffers a kind of indigestion. In
the process of promoting it to a mature and larger
discipline, we have tried to feed it with almost
everything that is directly or indirectly related
to it. Thus, during the past twenty years, we have
witnessed accounting being given a variety of diets,
including methodology, quantitative analysis, information systems, measurement theory, communication
theory, behavioral sciences, economics, political
science, mathematics, and philosophy. The most one
can say about accounting thinking at present is that
it is in a state of chaos or confusion. Consequently,
it is not a simple matter today to identify what

accounting actually is. Nevertheless, we shall try
to recapitulate, in a general way, some of the
various thoughts about the identity of the accounting
discipline.

*Accounting for internal users and accounting for
external users*—In recent years, the general area
of accounting has been divided into accounting for
internal users and accounting for external users.
It may be noted here that this was not the situation
in the early days when accounting was mainly for
internal purposes. The separation of management
from ownership, the emergence of large corporations,
legal requirements of accounting reports, diversified groups of users asking for different kinds of
information, information needed for management
planning and controlling purposes, and the influence
of management science have contributed to the division of accounting into two major subareas, namely,
management accounting and financial accounting. This
functional classification, however, does not, and
should not, affect the basic nature and function of
accounting. A crucial question often raised is:
Does this division mean that we would need two
separate theoretical structures—one for managerial
accounting and one for financial accounting? Some
would contend that a *general* framework of accounting,
when constructed, should be broad enough to cover
the whole area of accounting. A related question is
whether such a general, broad framework is feasible
or attainable.
The following discussion is a more serious one,

since it relates to the basic nature, meaning, and scope of accounting, and involves a number of controversial issues. One position is that accounting is an independent discipline. This may mean two things: Accounting, in its traditional sense, is a practical art, and thus it makes its own rules; or accounting is a scientific discipline, and it will have then its own formal theoretical structure. A different position held by some academicians is that accounting is not an independent discipline but is a subdivision of some large disciplines. Amid these various views, accounting has been identified in a number of ways.

Accounting is a branch of economics—In a broad sense, accounting has for years been regarded by some accountants as a branch of economics or, rather, a branch of applied economics; it has been said, with this in mind, that accounting should look upon economics as its master discipline. Whether this is a valid point of view is, of course, open to debate, but one probably cannot deny that there is a close relationship between accounting and economics. For one thing, a number of basic accounting concepts are derived from those in economics. For another, connections between the theory of the firm and the accounting firm-model (roughly speaking, the accounting entity), between microaccounting and macroaccounting, have been expounded repeatedly by both accountants and economists, as evidenced by the abundance of relevant literature. But the question still remains: Although intimately related, shall accounting be regarded as a branch of economics? *Accounting is an applied science*—The identification of accounting as an applied science actually places accounting in the area of the arts.[2] This is fine, except that, being an applied discipline, it must have a theoretical foundation upon which application takes place. This kind of argument may be extended to divide accounting into "pure accounting" and "applied accounting," or "academic accounting" and "practical accounting." These terms have appeared repeatedly in contemporary accounting literature. The message seems to be that accounting practice is in need of a theoretical framework. When we compare accounting with other professions, such as engineering and medicine, it is quite clear that the latter have their foundations in, say, mathematics, physics, chemistry, biology, and so forth, but that accounting operates without a conceptual framework. This seems to mean that, in order to be an independent discipline, accounting should be developed at two different levels— theoretical and applied. Without a formally constructed frame of reference, accounting will either remain an art or must rely on certain areas of formal learning as its master disciplines.

Accounting is an information system—Under this version, accounting is treated as a system of processing and transforming relevant information for guiding further action and decision making. Information theory is concerned primarily with defining and measuring the amount of information in a message. That there are a number of possible answers to a given problem suggests probabilities of various ways of solving the problem. Two sets of probabilities are noted—the one before the reception of relevant information and the other after it. Alternative answers are affected by the two sets of probabilities, because the amount of information conveyed before and after affects and induces changes of knowledge about the problem and its possible answers. The problem of identifying these two sets of probabilities is likely to be the most difficult one in the application of information theory, especially in the social sciences. Instead of measuring the amount and content of total information in a message, concepts of information theory may be applied to a context in which aggregates are analyzed by looking into their respective parts. It is in these kinds of "decomposition measures" that an application of information theory, which originated in physics, to certain social sciences (e.g., sociology, economics, management science, and possibly accounting) is made possible.

It is far from clear to what extent the information approach can be applied to accounting. Furthermore, we must not lose sight of the fact that accounting, when defined as an information system, is only a part of the general information system of an entity and that the kind of accounting information conveyed is necessarily determined and limited by the theoretical framework of accounting. Thus, treating accounting as an information system in the absence of a theoretical frame of reference is only treating it as a working scheme. No one would dispute the claim that accounting

produces information, but the validity and relevance
of accounting information are not rooted merely in
an operating scheme. Perhaps reactions from information receivers will make us reexamine, critically,
the foundations upon which accounting information
is accumulated.

Accounting is a measurement-communication discipline—
That accounting is a measurement-communication
discipline is probably the most widely held view
concerning the identity of accounting at the present
time. The involvement of measurement and communication
theories in accounting research is a fairly recent
endeavor. Because of the emphasis placed on measurement
in current accounting literature, further discussion
on this subject matter will be found in Chapter 6.
For our purpose in this chapter only general notations
are made.

All scientists engage in making measurements.
Briefly, measurement is concerned with the assignment
of symbols, usually numerical values, to objects,
events, or properties according to rule, in light of
relevant conceptual entities. The range of measurement extends from a simple classification to a full
measuring scale. The initial steps in measurement
are identification of the object and determination
of the *relevant* properties of the object to be
measured. The important questions at this stage
are: To what extent are the properties of the
object identifiable?   What are the relevant
properties?   Are these relevant properties
measurable?   The next step involves the establishment

of measurement rules and scales such as the selection
of a measurement system, ordering classes of objects,
and assignment of numerical values to objects or
properties.

Measurement is based on the premise that the
object in question is measurable or quantifiable,
which necessitates the formulation of *operational*
concepts. Concepts which are incapable of being
operationally defined are meaningless. Accordingly,
constitutive concepts must be converted into
operational ones for measurement purposes. Thus,
the measurement system is regarded as a basic
instrument of operationalism. The major difficulty
in measurement is not merely the finding of suitable
yardsticks, but rather the measurability of objects
or events.

Measurement may be regarded as a function of
accounting in the sense that the measurement process
permits quantification of accounting events. The
nature and meaning of accounting must be defined
outside the scales of measurement, because the
performance of measurement is an operating process
which necessarily functions within the theoretical
framework of the accounting discipline. Stated in
a general way, measurement without a theory is
"aimless wandering" and theory without measurement
is "mere speculation" or is "nonoperative."[3]

Communication is a process through which signs
or signals are transmitted from a source to a receiver.
In accounting, the range of the communication process
starts with observing and receiving relevant economic

events and extends to transmitting the resultant
information to users. To be effectively transmitted,
abstractions of events (e.g., words, numerical values,
and ratios) must be precisely derived by rigid
adherence to syntactical and semantical rules.
Communications require effective means and channels
so that the information being transmitted will not
be obscured or distorted. Of particular importance
is the ascertainment of the reactions and needs of
the receivers. In this respect, knowledge and tools
of the behavioral sciences are quite relevant in the
sense that they will aid in exploring motivations,
reactions, and needs of the accountant and of the
people using accounting reports.

Both measurement and communication exist within
a broad information system. The efficacy of an
information system depends primarily upon the
effectiveness and accuracy of measurement and
communication. For decision-making purposes, the
efficiency of the whole system rests upon the response
of the receiver as though he were directly exposed to
the events which were observed, measured, and reported
to him. At the present time, treating accounting
as a measurement-communication discipline is at most
in an infant stage, because the accountant has not
been either capable of mastering the essence of
measurement and communication theories and techniques
or able to apply them successfully to accounting.
Accounting is a part of general decision theories —
This view is essentially an extension of the one
regarding accounting as part of a general information

system to the point that accounting is treated as
a part of the more general decision theories.[4]
The holder of this viewpoint maintains that
accounting outputs are simply inputs to the decision
theories of both investment and management and that
the validity or usefulness of accounting information
hinges upon its relevance to decision models.
Accordingly, this view holds that there is no such
thing as theory confirmation in accounting; rather,
it is the decision theories that need confirmation.
This seems to imply that accounting is not and
cannot be a separate discipline of itself. It also
follows that the kind of accounting information
provided is necessarily determined and conditioned
by decision theories.

Accounting is a socioeconomic discipline—This is a
new viewpoint. As a matter of fact, it is so new
that we do not really know what socioeconomic
accounting is in terms of its nature and scope.
David Linowes defines it as ". . . the application
of accounting in the field of the social sciences.
These include sociology, political science, and
economics."[5] Sybil C. Mobley contends that socioeconomic accounting ". . . refers to the ordering,
measuring and analysis of the social and economic
consequences of governmental and entrepreneurial
behavior. . . . A measure limited to economic consequences is inadequate as an appraisal of the cause-
effect relationships of the total system; it neglects
the social effects."[6] From these quotes we see
that the vista of socioeconomic accounting is much

broader than any of the definitions of accounting
that we have previously known.   It demands the
kind of accounting information that will be used to
evaluate business and governmental activities in
terms of overall social well-being; and, as such,
accounting should be concerned with not only
economic effects but also social and political
consequences of such activities.   Thus the traditional market-based criterion of measurement must
be somehow implemented by "social measurement."   A
10 percent increase in GNP, for example, is not
necessarily an indication of "betteroffness" of the
society as a whole; rather, it should be analyzed
and measured in order to determine whether the
economic, social, and political well-being of the
various groups of the society is increased or
whether certain groups are better off at the expense
of the well-being of some other groups.

In general, it appears that the ultimate goal
of socioeconomic accounting is to deal almost with
the total socioeconomic environment of mankind—an
order so large that no known social science has
ever been able to fulfill it.   How we can expect
the accounting discipline to grow to the extent that
it will surpass all the other social sciences is a
question without answer at present.   Granted that
the idea of socioeconomic accounting is socially
desirable, socioeconomic accounting, in light of
its exceedingly broad scope, may have to be subdivided into, for instance, accounting for political
equity, accounting for social costs and benefits,

accounting for social responsibility and public
interest, accounting for social progress, environmental accounting, and so forth. In addition, traditional auditing may have to be extended in order
to include, say, "social and political audit." In
the final analysis, we hold that implementation of
any of these subdivisions requires, first, operationally defined social value concepts and, secondly,
an identification of relevant measurable properties
of these value concepts.

Accounting is a discipline of scientific study—
The foregoing discussion identifies accounting either
as a subject closely related to some larger disciplines
(e.g., economics and management science) or as a
system providing relevant information preconditioned
by the needs of specific groups of users of accounting
data. There is an ambitious view which holds that
accounting should be regarded as a branch of systematized learning and that it exists in its own right
in the sense that, like other sciences, it deals with
a part of the total environment. Specifically, this
view of accounting depicts certain aspects of the
interplay of human activities and scarce resources.
With or without specific users in mind, there is a
class of phenomena (and hence a body of data) arising
from possession and utilization of scarce resources;
accounting is simply a field of study which accounts
for these activities or human experiences in a
systematized manner, so as to provide explanations
for these past and present phenomena as well as to
anticipate future experience. Of course, accounting

is not the only discipline which deals with
this area of human activities. There are other disciplines which are concerned with this subject matter,
too. All these disciplines, including accounting,
are interrelated. But this does not mean that the
field of accounting coincides (though it may overlap)
with those of the other disciplines. The distinction
of a certain field of study rests upon its orientation, specific emphasis, and detailed description of
the subject matter involved.

Two significant features of this view are
neutrality and the absence of value judgment. Neutrality here means that no *specific* purposes for
providing accounting information are predetermined.
In other words, accounting is concerned, in a neutral
and objective manner, with certain aspects of human
activities. The user of the data so accumulated is
only incidental to the accounting discipline. Absence
of value judgment implies that observation and measurement of certain phenomena of the outside world are
without any value connotations. Save for the decision
to select the subject matter for study, to delineate
the scope of the study, and to adopt proper methodology,
value judgment is not a part of the theory structure
of accounting. In other words, matters relating to
desirable ends and efficiency of possession and utilization of economic resources resulting from human
motivation and behavior are not judged but are reported
as they are. Thus, evaluation and interpretation of
accounting information are left to users of the data.
Information so provided does establish a basis for
choice among alternatives (i.e., for further action

or decision making), but how the information is used
or interpreted is outside the domain of accounting.
It is quite clear that this view attempts to place
accounting in a scientific status with a minimum
amount of value content. Whether or not this view
is a valid one remains to be seen. A major advantage
of this version of accounting is that it will eliminate many of the controversial issues and handicaps
involved in the construction of an accounting theory
at the present time, such as user's needs, goal
determination, and other matters requiring value judgments (e.g., fair presentation and the auditor's
opinion). The obvious difficulty is that if accounting
becomes a science, it will be in the area of the social
sciences and may not be entirely value free.

It should be noted that the various versions of
the identity of the accounting discipline presented
above are not at all clear-cut. To some extent, many
of them are overlapping. It is clear that whatever
view is adopted, it will definitely condition and
shape the type and content of accounting theory.

A Broad Definition of Accounting and Its Relevance
to a General Structure of Accounting Theory

As stated, the various views about the identity
of accounting are not wholly distinctive among themselves. Each version signifies a degree of emphasis
on the nature, meaning, and function of accounting.
These various viewpoints also reflect, unmistakably,
the current state of accounting thinking. It may
also be noted here that some of the viewpoints may
lead to the construction of a general theory of
accounting, others to the formulation of special

accounting theories. This indicates that there will
be a number of theories, general or special, in the
area of the accounting discipline. Some of the theories
may be complementary; others may represent conflicting
views. Conflicting theories may make us aware that
one of them is valid or that a new theory or theories
may be needed to cope with a given situation. In
addition, a group of special theories often precedes
the arrival of a general theory. Ideally, these
various special theories of a given discipline will
eventually be synthesized so that a *general* theory
will emerge. Except in highly matured disciplines,
this ideal state is rarely attained, particularly in
the area of the social sciences. This means that,
for a discipline like accounting, we may have to live
with a variety of its identities and hence of its
theories. For our purposes here, however, it is
instructionally desirable to have a general definition of accounting. A general definition of identification will be extensive in range so that it will
allow room for the development of a broad, flexible
structure to accommodate a number of special theories
of accounting. With this understanding, we shall
identify accounting as: *a discipline which is concerned with the measurement and communication of
cerain aspects of the total environment relating to
the interplay of man and his possession and utilization of scarce means.*

The meaning of "discipline" (systematized
learning) was discussed in Chapter 2. Since all the
components of the total environment are interrelated,
the selection of certain aspects for study is largely a

matter of necessity and expediency. "Interplay of
man and scarce means" must be broadly interpreted,
including considerations given to human motivation
and behavior related to scarce resources, measurement
of relevant events, and communication of essential
information for guiding further action or anticipating
future experience.

The Extending Boundaries of the Accounting Discipline
Generally speaking, the extent of accounting
analysis is limited to economic events of specific
entities which, in a free-enterprise system, are
measured through the market mechanism or its equivalent. The magnitude of the accounting entity does
not necessarily alter the basic nature and meaning of
accounting, as long as the total environment within
which accounting functions remains unchanged. It has
come to the attention of the accountant in recent years
that the size of the accounting entity may range from
an individual firm to the economy as a whole. Thus,
within the general area of accounting, there are two
main subareas. One, which deals with economic events
of specific business enterprises or institutions, may
be labeled "microaccounting"; and the other, which
is concerned with aggregate economic measures, may
be called "macroaccounting." The magnitude of the
accounting unit itself is not a necessary condition
for measurement but merely an indication of the level
of quantification.

Reliance on the market criterion for measuring
activities, although highly valid, is neither inclusive nor conclusive. Its use is essentially
operational in nature and is attributed to a number

of factors, such as objectivity, factuality, measurability, and reliability. The market criterion for measurement purposes in accounting, however, is being used only to a limited extent. When fully employed, it will move us, for instance, from historical cost accounting to current value accounting. Because of the reliance on the market criterion, imputed transactions are generally excluded from financial accounting, but they could be recognized as equivalent transactions, as has been done in some of the segments of macroaccounting (e.g., national income accounting and input-output accounting).

Thus far, because of the lack of suitable yardsticks, we have not been able to apply the so-called welfare criterion for measuring economic activities in accounting. Without objective measuring units, the welfare or well-being criterion of measurement often becomes a matter of value judgment. There are, however, encouraging signs with respect to well-being measurement, such as the development of the cost-benefit approach. We certainly agree with the contention that, since accounting is concerned with providing relevant information with respect to the utilization of scarce resources, such information should be of interest to all members of the society who, upon receiving the information, will act to see that further allocation and utilization of economic resources should be directed toward maximization of benefits for the society as a whole. The fulfillment of this ultimate goal rests upon our ability to develop a set of relevant operational concepts and suitable measurement scales.

Of particular importance concerning the scope of accounting is the expansion of application of measureme methods in accounting. The 1964 Committee to Prepare a Statement of Basic Accounting Theory of the American Accounting Association recommended multidimensional reporting with emphasis placed on multivaluation measures, not only calling for the use of several measurement bases (i.e., historical costs, price-level adjustments, current costs, and current values) but also suggesting the use of nondeterministic measures or quantum ranges and probabilistic measures.[7] In addition, the Committee contended that multidimensional accounting would "involve measurement against more than one goal or objective such as profit object, goals of employees and consumers, and the national interest, where each possesses its own unit of measurement."[8]

The preceding discussion shows that the boundaries of accounting are extending in terms of the magnitude of the accounting unit, multivaluations, and measurement criteria. In addition, accounting is expanding in an interdisciplinary sense. Contemporary accounting literature reflects clearly the relevance and applicability of a number of other disciplines to accounting. When all are considered, it seems to make one wonder where accounting ends and other disciplines begin, and it may give the impression that accounting is losing its own identity. This mode of thinking, however, is not well founded. A discipline does not lose

its identity as long as its purpose and function
are precisely defined. (It may be noted here
that the purpose and function of a discipline and
its theoretical framework are functionally related.)
The state of confusion that exists in the accounting
discipline today stems largely from the fact that,
in terms of systematized learning, accounting is
a young discipline; it has to learn and borrow
heavily from other disciplines certain theoretical
constructs and techniques. It will take time to
sort and adapt them. Some of them may prove to be
relevant to accounting, others not. In addition,
we need to formulate our own constructs. This is
a very time-consuming process and it may take a
number of decades for the current chaotic situation
to clear up. We must be patient.

Empirical Research in Accounting

Although the accounting discipline is by
nature an empirical science, accounting is
distinctly lacking in empirical research. It has
been said that because accounting (like other
social sciences) is extremely limited with respect
to controlled experiments, the accounting theorist
must draw heavily from a set of basic propositions
and then rely on empirical studies to test the
deduced statements. While we are not so sure
about the first part of the assertion, we definitely
have no quarrel with the second part. In recent
years, some accountants have begun to pay attention
to the significance of empirical research.
Pioneering efforts in this respect are being made

largely by the Institute of Professional Accounting,
University of Chicago. In terms of theory confirmation,
however, we are not especially encouraged by these
kinds of empirical activities in accounting at the
present time—directed, by and large, at specific
items or events mostly in the form of simulations.

It should be stated that analytical research
and empirical work are complementary. The basic
idea of engaging in empirical study is to test or
verify hypotheses, models, or theories (existing
or newly formed). The fact that model building
often takes place prior to empirical testing
indicates that hypothesis or theory construction
is a prerequisite for empirical research. The
fruitfulness of a given empirical study depends
basically upon the elegance and meaningfulness of
the model or hypothesis being tested. Professor
Nil H. Hakansson[9] aptly states, "The problem
with putting good data in a garbage can is that
they smell like garbage when they are taken out."
There are, of course, instances where empirical
work may be done on observations in search of a
model, but this is not really the same as proving
or verifying a model or a hypothesis.[10] Thus,
two things can be said about empirical research.
First, empirical research is rarely employed as a
total approach for the construction of a theoretical
framework. Second, testing or verification through
empirical work is almost always partial. In any
event, empirical studies must be viewed as an
integral part of research methodology in accounting.
No meaningful accounting theory can be entirely

devoid of empirical verification. Empirical studies
will not only increase (or decrease) our confidence
in a given theory but will also reduce the often
fruitless debate on the validity of deductively
derived propositions. A theory may be entirely
valid in a logical sense, but it may be tautological.
For instance, it is true that generally accepted
accounting principles (GAAP) do not have formal structure
or that they lack logical consistency, but a
logical structure could be built for generally
accepted accounting principles as attempted
by Yuji Ijiri using an axiomatic approach.[11]
This, however, does not necessarily make GAAP a
valid frame of reference for providing relevant
and meaningful accounting information. With or
without a formal structure, the meaningfulness of
GAAP should be examined through extensive empirical
research. The process of a scientific inquiry is
incomplete without empirical studies. It is beside
the point to assert that empirical research can
never provide complete testing or verification of
theories, because in scientific inquiries we do
not, and cannot, seek such an ideal state. The
strength of empirical research lies in its reassuring
us, although always on a partial basis, as to our
theoretical position.

     As a final note, it should be stated that
empirical research and empirical testing are not,
at all, synonymous; the former emerges at various
stages of the entire process of a scientific study
and the latter represents the final phase of the
study. Those who contend that theory (or model)

construction requires no empirical imports
simply reveal their misconception of the scientific
method. The "back-and-forth-movement" pattern
of research in any empirical discipline signifies
that we are constantly *guided* by the experiential
world and are in need of constant assurance from
it.

[1]Thomas R. Prince, *Extension of the Boundaries of of Accounting Theory* (South-Western Publishing Co., 1963), p. 13.

[2]Dwight P. Flanders, "Accountancy, Systematized Learning, and Economics," *The Accounting Review,* (October 1961): 564-76.

[3]Robert R. Sterling, "On Theory Construction and Verification," *The Accounting Review,* (July 1970): 455.

[4]Ibid., pp. 454-6.

[5]David F. Linowes, "Socioeconomic Accounting," *The Journal of Accountancy,* (November 1968): 37.

[6]Sybil C. Mobley, "The Challenges of Socioeconomic Accounting," *The Accounting Review,* (October 1970); 762-63.

[7]*A Statement of Basic Accounting Theory* (Chicago: American Accounting Association, 1966), p. 65.

[8]Ibid.

[9]Nil H. Hakansson, "Empirical Research in Accounting, 1960-70: An Appraisal," *Accounting Research 1960-70: A Critical Evaluation* ed. Nicholas Dopuch and Lawrence Revsine (Urbana: Center for International Education and Research in Accounting, University of Illinois, 1973), p. 157.

[10]This point was well put by Hector R. Anton. See his "Critical Synthesis of Conference Papers," *Empirical Research in Accounting: Selected Studies, 1968* (Chicago: The Institute of Professional Accounting, Graduate School of Business, University of Chicago, 1969), p. 167.

[11]Yuji Ijiri, *The Foundations of Accounting Measurement* (Englewood Cliffs, New Jersey: Prentice-Hall, Inc., 1967).

4 The Nature, Meaning, and Epistemological Foundation of Accounting Propositions

Ever since 1955,[1] numerous issues have been raised with respect to the basic nature, meaning, and function of accounting, but none has been satisfactorily answered. To say that current accounting thinking is confusing is an understatement. We contend, however, that this is a healthy symptom in the sense that accounting, though an ancient art, appears to be emerging as a scientific discipline. Many of the issues are centered around the meaningfulness of accounting information resulting in extensive research efforts by prominent students of the accounting discipline. These efforts have produced the conclusion shared by many accountants, mostly academicians, that basically the validity and meaningfulness of accounting information hinge upon the soundness of a frame of reference for accounting in terms of logical rigor and empirical correspondence and that accounting, at present, does not have such a conceptual framework.

The major task of theory construction is to put together the building blocks in a systematic manner. But what are the building blocks? Simply put, they are classes of propositions. Thus, we may say that a theory comprises a set of classes of propositions assembled in an orderly manner; the essence of systematized learning can most effectively be identified by examining the basic nature and meaning of its propositions in general and the various classes of propositions contained in its structure and their relations in particular. Accordingly, a discourse on the theory structure of accounting will naturally call for an exploration of the nature and meaning of accounting propositions, and this is the purpose of the present chapter.

What is a Proposition?

A proposition is a declarative or indicative sentence which has a truth value (i.e., either true or false, logically or empirically). A question, a command, an imperative sentence, or a statement expressing a wish, is not a proposition, because what is asked, commanded, or wished makes no commitment as to truth or falsity. Like those in many other sciences, propositions which constitute the theoretical structure of the accounting discipline include postulates, constructs, definitions, hypotheses, and deduced propositions or generalized statements. First, the nature and meaning of each of these classes of propositions must be identified and defined. Next comes the important task of

explicating the formal relationships of the propositions within each class and between classes.
The final step is to put them together in an orderly
way, that is, to have a formal structure for them.

Analytic and Synthetic Propositions

The formulation of a proposition is a manner
of acquiring knowledge for asserting, affirming, or
denying our beliefs. Epistemologically, propositions
are of two types: "analytic" and "synthetic". Propositions whose truth values can be identified by
analyzing the meaning of the words used are called
analytic. Propositions which have factual content
are called synthetic. There are two important
terms which are closely associated with analytic
and synthetic—a priori and a posteriori.[2] The
former refers to the type of propositions for which
truth values can be shown by pure *reason*, and the
latter denotes the kind of propositions for which
truth values can be decided only after facts are
available.

Modern empiricists, in ascribing to David
Hume's doctrine, advocate that all analytic propositions are a priori and, hence, are tautologies,
and all synthetic propositions are a posteriori
and hence are "hypotheses."[3] The elegance of
tautology is that it is so inclusive as to leave
nothing unsaid. As such, a priori statements are
noted for their certainty, and the test of their
truths is purely formal; but, to extreme logical
positivists, they are meaningless because they
lack factual content. On the other hand, the

truth criterion for synthetic propositions is not
a formal but a material one. Synthetic propositions
have factual content; so their truths are not
guaranteed and thus are always probable. Most
Kantians and those of the post-Kantian idealist
tradition have asserted that there can be a synthetic
judgment a priori. Logical empiricists, however,
have ruled out any propositions that can be either
analytic a posteriori or synthetic a priori. They
maintain that propositions are of either the
analytic a priori type or the synthetic a posteriori
type, and that there cannot be any propositions that
fall into categories between these two types. Propositions which do not satisfy either class are held
to be metaphysical which, according to the logical
empiricists, are senseless.

The classification of propositions is critical.
While philosophers have been in constant feud over
the problems of the a priori (analytic) and the a
posteriori (synthetic) classification of propositions,
"... no criteria of analytic and synthetic seem to
maintain the sharp dualism."[4] The mind-and-matter
issue is far from being settled. Irrespective of
their nature, not all synthetic propositions are
practically verifiable. On the other hand, it is
doubtful whether we can do away entirely with all
analytic propositions in any scientific inquiry,
because absence of some analytic elements may lead
to logical difficulties (e.g., order and relation).
Ludwig von Mises advocates that the cognitive
value of a priori knowledge is as indispensable
for the human mind as is the distinction between

A and non-A.[5] John G. Kemeny says: "While in a
sense mathematics brings us nothing new, since it
does no more than analyze the meaning of our words,
it brings us facts that are *new to us*, facts we did
not realize we possessed."[6] In addition, "tautologies"
are sometimes necessary for serving us in our empirical
search for knowledge. As A. C. Ewing puts it,
"... some a priori principle about the world is
required if induction is to be justified."[7]

   The issue relative to the analytic and the
synthetic not only brings out the conflict between
rationalists and empiricists but may also be regarded
as an indicator of the traditional feud between
deduction and induction. The traditional rationalist
will assert that our beliefs from pure reason,
processed through deductive reasoning, can arrive
at knowledge of the world without being verified
by experience. In contrast, the empiricist will
assert that all beliefs are not only derived from
experience but must be verified, or verifiable.
These are extreme positions. Rarely is the use of
the deductive or inductive method so pure that
either one excludes, in toto, the other. The
difficulty in isolating inductive reasoning from
deductive reasoning is just as great as excluding
analytic elements from empirical inquiries. As
Alfred Jules Ayer puts it:

> The process by which scientific theories
> come into being is often deductive rather
> than inductive. The scientist does not
> formulate his laws only as the result of
> seeing them exemplified in particular
> cases. Sometimes he considers the

> possibility of the law before he is in
> possession of the evidence which justifies
> it.... He does not, as Hume implied,
> passively wait for nature to instruct him;
> rather, as Kant saw, does he force nature
> to answer the questions which he puts to
> her. So that there is a sense in which
> the rationalists are right in asserting
> that the mind is active in knowledge...
> it is true that the activity of theorizing
> is, in its subjective aspect, a creative
> activity, and that the psychological
> theories of empiricists concerning "the
> origins of our knowledge" are vitiated
> by their failure to take this into
> account.[8]

The epistemological criteria of knowledge are
indeed difficult to resolve. The current state of
philosophy is as critical as ever. Pending further
breakthrough, we hold that all human knowledge is
fragmentary because of its partial character.
Although we must leave those issues to philosophers,
accounting—as a branch of learning—cannot escape the
fundamental tenets of philosophy and methodology.
The search for a theoretical framework of accounting
necessitates formulation of propositions. An
explication of the implications of a set of
propositions, particularly of those which are labeled
primitives and hypotheses, calls for deductive
reasoning. On the other hand, accounting, unlike
mathematics and logic, is a demonstrative discipline.
When an accounting proposition is accepted as a priori,
it does not necessarily mean that this proposition
has no empirical root but, rather, it is accepted
mainly for methodological reasons. In addition,
the validity and meaningfulness of accounting
hypotheses or theories must be supported ultimately

by consequential operations or proof. In the final
analysis, one may say that there are no *final*
propositions in a scientific inquiry.

The Nature, Meaning, Formulation, and Functions of
Primitive Propositions of Accounting

     Through the years, accountants have used, as
the foundation for theory formulation, a variety
of terms to denote a set of basic propositions,
such as "basic concepts," "assumptions," "postulates,"
"primitives," "premises," "axioms," and "principles."
Some of these terms carry about the same connotation;
others differ in both conceptual and technical
aspects. In addition, we have found, in a number
of certain occasions, the inclusion of value statements
in a set of basic propositions. In general, they
all are intended to be a class of statements which
are supposed to support a conclusion or from which
other propositions are inferred. It may be noted here
that for most empirical disciplines, no one category
of basic statements is sufficient. Some initial
propositions are empirical statements, others are
postulated statements, and still others are
conclusions from separate systems or disciplines.
With this understanding, let us explore the basic
nature, meaning, and function of accounting postulates.
We wish to note, methodologically, that it is not
always necessary to have a set of *explicit* premises
to start an inquiry.

     First, accounting, by nature, is an empirical
science, and as such its propositions, including
primitive propositions, cannot be purely a priori
or analytic, that is, unlike those in mathematics

and logic which have no connections whatsoever with
the empirical world. This, of course, does not
mean that accounting has no use for "theoretical
constructs," which, as will be discussed later,
lack immediate empirical correspondence. On the
contrary, they provide the basic strength of any
highly developed theory (in terms of infiniteness)
and are needed as placeholders for "empirical
concepts." In addition, postulated statements are
almost always needed in a set of basic propositions,
because absence of this type of statement will lead
to complications and difficulties in theory construction.
With respect to the degree of empirical content (i.e.,
high or low) of a synthetic proposition, as well as
the *level* of the theory under construction, it is
the theorist's privilege to decide. Although an a
posteriori or synthetic proposition is based upon
past and present experiences which provide a degree
of assurance for anticipating future experience, the
reliance on empirical correspondence is not a guarantee.
It is true that we cannot learn from the future, which
does not exist, and that we must respect a great
deal of the past, from which we hope to ascertain
our present position so that we can continue. The
past, however, as well as the present, may not be
clear or sufficient to provide us with all the
information that we would like to have. In a sense,
we are caught between the present and the future.
This is a dilemma and there is no satisfactory solution
to this situation.

    Second, the acceptance of a set of basic

propositions of accounting as a priori is made in a methodlogical sense. This is ncessary because we need a starting point or a place to stand. In other words, a set of primitives identifies the initial position from which we proceed; it sets forth the basic conditions or boundaries within which the inquiry is conducted.

Third, although we say that postulates are "unproved," eventually they may be "proved" (or disproved) in an indirect way, as occurs when the deduced propositions are validated or invalidated— although always on a partial basis—by empirical verification. When they are invalidated, we may have to go back to our initial propositions and reexamine them.

Fourth, the seeming simplicity of a postulate, the formation of which is either a matter of abstraction resulting from simplification of reality or is an invention by the theorist in light of his knowledge and prior experience, may give an unrealistic appearance and can be quite deceptive. So far as theory construction is concerned, this unrealistic feature of postulates need not bother us too much. One must not commit the methodological fallacy, however, that postulates and their empirical referents, if any, correspond in a concrete, immediate manner. They are not, and probably never will be, largely due to the process of abstraction, construction, and interpretation of the particulars in the formulation of such postulates.

Fifth, one may not say more than what is implied in a postulate, for the rules of logic would not allow us to do so.

Sixth, that a given set of postulates describes
or carves out only certain aspects of the total
environment marks off the boundaries of the inquiry
in question. The researcher must select only those
postulates which are most relevant to his study. This
is a matter not only of expediency but also of necessity
otherwise, the researcher would in no time get himself
tangled up with the *total* set of relationships of the
environment which is an impossible task for anyone.[9]

Seventh, a theory can be validly interpreted and
applied only within the setting prescribed by its ad
initium propositions; which is extremely important,
because a theory, as stated previously, is not without
boundaries or limitations. The inclusion of an
additional postulate may enlarge or contract the origina
foundation. A change of setting may render an existing
theory incompetent or obsolete. Thus we must not apply
a theory to a situation which, in the first place, is
not implied by its postulates.

Eighth, from the preceding statement, it is clear
that the selection of a set of postulates requires
preliminary identification of the setting of a theory
structure through either observation or presupposition.
In addition, although the implications of a set of
postulates are not immediately known, each postulate
must be stated explicitly and its terms must be
defined precisely. This is a very crucial point in the
sense that the derivation of initial propositions, as
well as subsequent propositions (hypotheses and theories
is often constrained by our inability to cope effectivel
with the complexity of the interdependence of human
actions and the circumscribed environment, compounded

by the factor of uncertainty.

Ninth, in terms of coherence, the frequently
mentioned notion that accounting postulates are
"open-ended" is fallacious when applied to a *given*
theory structure. This, of course, does not mean
that the general area of accounting is a closed
system.

Tenth, since, in general, accounting studies
the interaction of human motivation and behavior
and scarce means, the search for accounting postulates
must go beyond the traditional boundaries of accounting.
In other words, they are necessarily selected from
those aspects of the socioeconomic environment of
mankind that are of relevance to the accounting
discipline.

Eleventh, that accounting postulates are
derived basically from the socioeconomic environment
signifies that some of the postulates reflect certain
human ideas, which are necessarily conditioned by
prior experience and often contain an element of
imagination. In the formulation of a postulate,
however, we had better be careful with the element
of imagination, which, when carried too far, may
become speculation. A sound theory should not be
built on a speculative, shaky foundation.

Finally, it may be mentioned that the scientist
prefers "simplicity." Other things being equal, he
will always select simple postulates or concepts over
complex ones. Although there is no definite number
of postulates for a given inquiry, the scientist is,
for obvious reasons, always in favor of keeping the

number to a minimum. The ability to select only relevant ones and discard irrelevant ones often reflects the researcher's proficient skills and knowledge in his own field. In this respect, however, we can take comfort from the fact that for a given area the number of basic postulates is usually small (for one thing, postulates are broad in nature, and for another the inclusion of constraints or purely assumed statements in a set of postulates stabilizes the area of study in question) and that irrelevant ones which may have been included are often discovered and then discarded in subsequent operations.

The Notion "Self-Evidence" and Accounting Postulates

Accountants have been quite remiss in the formulation and selection of basic postulates. Some of the existing accounting postulates are the results of purely perceptual experience relative to specific circumstances; others are heavily loaded with allegedly factual evidences or value connotations. Still others are statements loosely postulated in the light of expediency and convenience. In general, accounting postulates are deficient in clarity and coherence. Although there seems to be a consensus among accountants that basic accounting postulates are derived largely from the environment in which accounting functions, one of the most disturbing notions about accounting postulates is that accountants have often— as a matter of fact, too often—taken a set of postulates, whatever it is, for granted without serious attempt to explicate their nature, meaning, and relationships. Thus, accounting postulates have been mistakenly labeled

as "self-evident," "certain," and "imperative," as
if they were simple, obvious facts or indubitable
truths. Whether this is intentional or unintentional,
the consequence is a state of ambiguity and confusion
which has caused much misconception in following
through those postulates at both the theoretical
and the practical levels.

Because accounting by nature is an empirical
discipline, its postulates are only probably true and
need to be reevaluated continually; however, a stopping
point must be made in order to have a starting point
for an inquiry. A set of postulates is tentatively
accepted as valid only after a process of abstraction
and construction. The meaningfulness of conclusions
of a study is determined not so much by the logical
form or structure that is taken but by what is said
in the initial propositions or hypotheses; therefore,
we must deemphasize or, better, do away with, the
"self-evident" notion about accounting postulates.
If a self-evident statement means indubitable truth,
true by its own justification, or known immediately
to be true, then we must say that no such class of
propositions has been found in accounting. Self-
evident statements are not relative truths, but
necessary, absolute, certain truths. Philosophers
have attempted to uproot the meaning and origin of
self-evident truths. St. Thomas Aquinas regards
them as known immediately upon the knowledge of their
terms; Descartes thought that he had found a self-
evident truth in *Cogito, ergo sum.* (I think, therefore,
I am); Aristotle claims that self-evident truths
come from man's special faculty of insight or

intuition to grasp them; John Locke says that they
are derived from a person's reason (i.e., to know them
without proof); Aquinas and Descartes attribute them
to principles implanted in us by God; Benedict de
Spinoza finds them in the very nature of everything
that is; and some contemporary philosophers believe
that they are a matter of rules of grammar.
Irrespective of the merit or validity of each of the
philosophical versions of "self-evidence," the
point has been made——that is, none is relevant to the
basic nature of accounting postulates. As a matter
of fact, the history of science has repeatedly shown
that the so-called self-evident statements often
have turned out to be most questionable.

Definition

Words, terms, and symbols have no natural
meaning; meanings must be assigned to them. In
scientific study, it is paramount that no relevant
terms and concepts employed in the inquiry are left
in an ambiguous state. Failure to provide precise
definitions for the terms and concepts used will
lead to inaccurate thinking, confusion, and misunderstanding in subsequent operations. Definition is a
process of giving meanings to the terms and concepts
or clarifying them to make them precise. Logically,
they intend to expose the structure of a concept,
the result of which is also called a definition.

Definition is a complex controversial issue, and
logicians and philosophers have not yet come to a
complete agreement as to names, types, classifications,
and meanings of definition. No effort is made here

to offer a theory of definition. Rather, we wish
to expound briefly the nature and functions of
definitions, together with an identification of
some of the basic problems, so that we will be very
careful with the meaning of our terms and concepts
in a formal inquiry.[10]

Definitions are of many kinds, but they can be
reduced to the following form:

Definiendum = Definiens

where *definiendum* refers to a specific expression
of a given term being defined and *definiens* is an
expression which states or analyzes the meaning of
the definiendum. One familiar, and yet important,
distinction is made between "nominal" and "real"
definitions. In *Principia Mathematica*, Whitehead
and Russell place a nominal definition in the
following form:

Definiendum = Definiens Df.

where "Df." may be read "is, by definition, to be
equal in meaning." Thus, *implication* is symbolically
defined as follows:

$$p \supset q = p' \lor q. \text{ df.}$$

which means in words "p implies q" is equivalent by
definition to "not p or q." Under a nominal (also
called verbal) definition, the definiendum is to
have no meaning other than the definiens whose
meaning is already established; and, as such, it is
a stipulation. In other words, a nominal definition
offers merely an alternative expression or name but
equal in meaning to the definiens. A real definition
is a statement which brings out the essential nature

or attributes of some entity. A classical example
of searching for a real definition is found in
Plato's dialogue, "Euthyphro," where Socrates
questions Euthyphro about the meaning of piety.[11]
Socrates is trying to find a real definition of piety,
but the dialogue ends without finding a satisfactory
answer. A real definition is a genuine proposition.
Both the definiendum and the definiens have an
independent meaning. The definition is said to be
true if both of these meanings are equivalent (i.e.,
if such and such conditions are satisfied in defining
the given entity); it is false, if they are not.
Thus, real definitions have a "truth value," they
can serve as premises of an argument. Nominal definitions, whose meanings depend upon the definiens which is
separately determined, cannot be said to be true
or false; so they cannot be real premises of any
argument. The distinction between nominal and real
definitions, though important, however, cannot
always be maintained, since a nominal definition
often has some reference to a meaning analysis of
the words used.

The use of the expression "essential natures"
or "essential attributes" for identifying real
definitions is undoubtedly vague. To avoid such an
ambiguous expression, one may reinterpret the meaning
of some entity either in terms of meaning analysis
or by searching for an empirical explanation. This
does not mean that we can always have a real definition
for every entity that we encounter. Indeed, there are
numerous entities that defy our attempt to provide

meaningful definitions simply due to the fact that
we do not know what they are except perhaps intuitively.
In addition, short of ultimate answers or knowledge
of all the terms and concepts of which we are aware,
we may have to leave some of them undefined or have
them defined in a circular way. Empirical analysis
for the quest of a real definition requires reference
to empirical evidence. With respect to "meaning
analysis" (or "analytical definition"), like a
nominal definition, it is a matter of an analysis
of linguistic expressions. As opposed to a nominal
definition which presents a "new" expression by
stipulation, a meaning analysis, however, deals with
an expression already in use (called by Hempel the
analysandum) and produces a synonymous expression
(labeled by Hempel the *analysans*) which must be
understood previously.[12] The truth value of an
analytic definition rests upon whether or not its
analysans is synonymous with its *analysandum*. The
problem of using any given natural language in
analytical definitions is the complaint of vagueness
and disagreement among speakers of the language about
the meaning of the words used. Of course, this is
also true for nominal definitions and other kinds
of definitions. In scientific research, we need
precise definitions, in terms of determinacy and
uniformity, which call for the development of
artificial languages. Physics, for instance, would
not have advanced to its present state had it expressed
its basic terms ("force," "energy," "field," etc.)
in natural language. In addition, both analytical

and nominal definitions call for a clear indication
of their syntactical status in the expression being
defined (i.e., the logic form in which the term is
to be defined). The use of the subject-predicate
type of sentences in traditional logic for definitions
requires the interpretation of all predicates as
property (or class) terms (i.e., definitions by
the *genus* and *differentia* form where the genus is a
"class" and the differentia distinguishes one species
from another in the same *genus*; for example,
"Man is a rational animal" where the *genus* is
"animal" and the differentia is "rational.")
In scientific research, however, it is extremely
fruitful to have an expression defined (or explicated)
in *relation* and *function* terms, that is, supplemented
at least by two expressions referring to the same
term being defined. This is one of the two major
reasons why dictionary definitions which are mostly
expressed in property terms are unsuitable for
hypotheses or theory formation. The other is, of
course, the circularity of dictionary definitions.
Real definitions are often implicit, taking the form
of axioms or primitive propositions in scientific
inquiry.

That nominal definitions introduce "new" or
alternative expressions of the definiens (something
already defined through real definitions) is not a
trivial matter. On the contrary, it facilitates
the process of formal research, because a nominal
definition simplifies the already understood
properties of a given entity by giving it a "name"

or by symbolizing it. The use of symbols or
neutral words also have the advantage of doing away
with words having emotive connotations. Indeed if
in any scientific writing which makes no use of
nominal definitions, a term had to be expressed in
real or primitive terms everytime it was used, it
would make the material totally unintelligible. We
cannot have all the terms of a given system defined
in a nominal manner, however, because to do so would
result in an infinite regress or circularity which
is inadmissible in scientific studies. Thus, to
avoid circularity, nominal definitions have to be
introduced by means of *primitives* which are not
defined within the system, although special meanings
can be assigned to them within the system (e.g.,
the application of point and straight line of the
Euclidean geometry to physics requires an assignment
of meanings to them, for physics does not deal with
point and straight line per se). In this way, all
nominal definitions can be eliminated in terms of
the primitive terms. In other words, the definitional
chain of a given system must come to an end. In
addition to avoiding circularity, the above requirements
of nominal definitions preclude the possibility of
assigning two different definitions to the same term.

Within the contexts of real and nominal definitions,
philosophers differ on the classification and the
number of types which are too numerous to be considered
here. Of particular interest to the empirical science
is the so-called operational definition
by P. W. Bridgman in the 1920s. According to
Bridgman, the basic idea of operationism which calls

for the use of operating definitions is "the demand
that the concepts or terms used in the description
of experience be framed in terms of operations which
can be unequivocally performed."[13] To the operationist
any definition short of this idea is meaningless.
Operational definitions will be considered further
in the following section.

Precise definitions are of utmost importance
to concept development and theory formation; both
are intimately interrelated. Although definition
in terms of types, classifications, and essence is
still a controversial issue among philosophers and
logicians, every theorist should be fully aware of
the significance of the definitional issue in formal
inquiry. Accountants are lax in defining terms and
concepts of the accounting discipline, not so much
in the contention that we need more terms and
concepts but largely in that we have failed to define
rigorously those we already have. Since most accounting
terms and concepts have their roots in some much more
basic disciplines, it follows that, in addition to
their economy and expediency, nominal definitions
will find extensive usage in accounting. Modifications
of terms and concepts borrowed from those other
disciplines are, of course, a necessity. For "pure"
accounting constructs, which may be few in number,
we will require the use of real definitions. In
brief, we need to assign explicit, precise meanings
(empirical, analytical, or nominal) to the terms that
we employ, particularly in terms of relation and
function. To define, for instance, the term "assets"

as "things of value or economic resources owned"
is not much help unless we have a good understanding
of the characteristics, relationships, and functions
of the expressions stated in the definiens. In
addition, we have the habit of defining terms and
concepts broadly. The message is this: Define,
not a concept in toto (unless by doing so it can be
theoretically and operationally executed) but the
specific properties of a concept. Defining
"accounting income" as a "residual" amount is a good
example of the point just made. When we say "residual,"
we are saying something in the most ambiguous fashion.
We need to spell out, in a precise manner, the specific
elements and their relations which constitute the
residuum.

Concept

Every discipline is based upon certain fundamental concepts. They are basic ideas about the
world in which we live and serve as a base upon
which hypotheses and theories are inferred. It has
been said that new concepts are the work of a genius
or are discovered by intuition. Since we know little
about the mind of a genius, plus the fact that
intuition can be quite deceptive, we shall consider,
in a general way, how basic concepts are *formulated*.
Concept Formulation—A concept is the product of
connecting certain aspects of the external world
with the mind through sense experience and a process
of abstraction and construction. Phenomena of the
outside world are meaningless unless we can assign
meanings or forms to them. The meanings or forms

assigned reflect our understanding of the phenomena
observed. The process usually starts with perceiving
particulars. The variety of particulars of the
existential world is sorted out by a process of
classification, resulting in classes or "kinds" of
phenomena. This is facilitated by applying the
"similarity" principle, which is indispensable to
any scientific inquiry or knowledge acquisition.
Indeed, if we begin to look for "dissimilarities"
of a class of particulars, knowledge acquisition
would become an impossible task. For example,
one probably will never find two identical blades
of the grass in his lawn. Were one to proceed in
this way, he would end up by assigning a form,
meaning, or name to each blade of grass without
ever knowing the basic attributes of grass, and when
he saw other people's lawns, he would have to start
the same process over again.

Concept formulation goes through the process
both of observation and abstraction, as well as an
application of deductive logic. Initially, a
concept may be in the form of a vague notion about
a few individual instances. This primitive observation
may be called "protocol experience"; however, nothing
is learned from a single occurrence, or a few,
for no concrete basis for inferences is provided.
similar experience accumulates, we are beginning to
become familiar with a certain type of phenomena.
As the process goes on, our understanding of that
particular class of phenomena will increase to the
extent that it reflects a fairly clear idea about
the group of particulars in terms of their relations.

Pure sense experience, however, is insufficient for logical inferences. Our perception, notion, or idea about the empirical contents or concrete shapes of the particulars being observed or conceived must be distilled through a process of abstraction so that their common attributes can be identified. The abstraction process paves the way for subsequent explication of their relations and implications.

Diagram 4-1 shows the process of concept formulation. It starts with observation of specific or individual instances. The next step shows a state of *conception*—a mental image of observed results, which we may term "percept." According to Peter Caws, a deliberately changed or modified concept (i.e., concept at the perceptual state—percept) becomes a construct, "and a scientific construct, in particular, is a concept deliberately modified or invented with a view to erecting or improving a theory."[14] Kermit D. Larson suggested three stages of concept development—perceptual, conceptual, and constructural.[15] The seeming clarity and orderliness of these three. stages are flimsy, however, because there are no clear-cut boundaries between perception and conception.[16] In addition, the process of concept formulation involves a back-and-forth movement. Larson labels the process of refining a percept into a concept as "explanation," which, upon further development, results in "explication" (construct).[17] This process parallels Rudolf Carnap's procedure of explication which involves "the transformation of an inexact, prescientific concept, the *explicandum*, into a new,

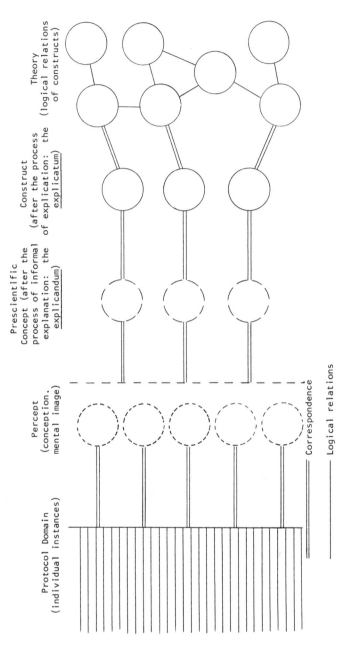

Diagram 4-1

Concept Development
(leading to theory construction)

exact concept, the *explicatum*."[18] Carnap sets forth
the following criteria for a construct: (1) similarity
to the *explicandum*, (2) exactness, (3) fruitfulness,
and (4) simplicity.[19] In brief, scientific or formal
concepts are *abstracted* forms derived from experience
through the process of explication and are apart
from any tangible contents or concrete integuments.
*Theoretical constructs, empirical concepts, and
operational concepts* — The formulation of a scientific
concept necessitates formalization of its constituent
attributes and relationships. The ultimate purpose
of a concept, however, is that it will function in
subsequent operations. Thus, to the operationalist,
the formalization of its attributes and their
relationships, is simply to set forth its operative
capacity.

A distinction should be made between theoretical
constructs and empirical constructs. It has been
said that theoretical or pure constructs are based on
imagination, postulation, and pure reason without any
trace of empirical correspondence. In a logical sense,
they possess the characteristics of purity and exactness
and are the result of an active exercise of the mind.
Empirical concepts, on the other hand, have their roots
in the protocol domain, sensory observations, and
experiences and are almost always impure, inexact,
and somewhat uncertain. The contrast between pure
constructs and empirical constructs just described,
however, is overstated. Rarely is a concept so pure
that it dissociates entirely from the outside world.
For theorization, both theoretical constructs and

empirical concepts serve as powerful bases. Although
empirical constructs are necessary to connect
theoretical operations and the external world,
theoretical constructs are needed to explain or validate
empirical constructs and, most of all, to provide the
kind of basic strength that a theory must have—namely,
infiniteness.

It has been said that in a scientific inquiry,
all concepts must be relevant to subsequent operations
in terms of measurement. A constitutive concept may
be highly valid conceptually but nonoperative in the
sense that its properties are immeasurable. There are
often several concepts about an object. For operational
purposes, the one that is selected may contain a
relatively low degree of purity and abstraction. For
instance, there are a number of income concepts, such
as psychic income, economic income, business income,
real income, money income, realizable income, realized
income, and taxable income. Some of these concepts
are operational, others are not. Those which are
operational vary in degree of purity and abstraction.
The significance of operational concepts has long been
visualized by the physical scientist who experienced
the difficulty of using pure constructs in experimentati
The turning point was made by P. W. Bridgman, the
foremost advocate of operationalism, who, in 1927,
claimed that meaningful concepts must relate to an
operational mode of thinking and must be adopted in
all fields of inquiry.[20] In essence, operationalism
appeals to experience and verification. Since the
number of operations in any experiment is infinite,

one may have to stop at a point where approximations
(through measurement) are reached. Approximations,
however, can never be substitutes in full for
theoretical constructs which have the property of an
infinite order. It has been said that strict followers
of operationalism can produce only "low-level
generalizations," which require more than operational,
empirical content.[21] Debate on the merit of
operationalism is not likely to be settled. Students
of accounting theory should be aware of the operational
mode of thinking, which undoubtedly will carry considerable
weight in the formulation of accounting theory. Strict
adherence to the operationalistic mode of thought,
however, may lead to a fallacious version of the true
nature and meaning of "theoretical constructs." Let
us see why this may be the case.

The contention that, in empirical science, all
theoretical constructs must be totally defined or
explicated in observation terms reflects a narrower
version of empiricism. In the first place, properties
of disposition terms (e.g., magnetic) are not
subject to direct observation; or at most the observ-
ableness of these properties is problematic, because in
essence each of them designates a disposition to display
specific reactions under certain specified conditions.
In the second place, certain basic concepts (e.g.,
length, mass) used for quantitative terms cannot
be defined fully in terms of observables. In addition,
the theoretical range of values (in terms of real-
number values) based on a certain basic concept is
infinite and has the power of continuum, whereas
the number of observations, no matter how large, is

finite. This implies further that the number of
observable characteristics and the number of
complexes formed out of them are finite as well.
Also, the use of the concepts and principles of
higher mathematics in the construction of scientific
theories would be impossible if we insisted on stating
all of the constructs in observation terms. What we
are trying to emphasize is that theoretical constructs
cannot be fully reduced to observation terms, although
the latter substantiate the former. It is exactly
in this sense that theoretical constructs are truly
fruitful or resourceful concepts.

    Theoretical constructs are the basis for general
laws and theories, which cannot be *fully* formulated
by empirical observations and measurements because
of their finite nature. While theoretical constructs
need empirical import to substantiate their validity,
the advancement of empirical theories, in the final
analysis, hinges upon the degree of theoretical import
which has the characteristics of determinacy and
uniformity. Two questions would, sooner or later,
be raised. One is: why in the first place does an
empirical discipline need theoretical constructs?
The other is: although empirical concepts correspond,
in a general way, and explain a given class of
particulars (phenomena), what explains the empirical
concepts in question? The answer to the first question
is that the infinite order of a theory is rooted in
its theoretical constructs. The answer to the second
question is that empirical concepts are guided and
illuminated by relevant theoretical constructs. A

few examples will clarify the point in question.
The dollar is, in a manner of speaking, a theoretical
construct; it does not refer to the specific dollars
that anyone has, and it would be an endless process
to count the number of dollars that individuals
possess. Similarly, "the firm" of the "theory of
the firm" is a theoretical construct; and the accounting
entity is another one. When we speak of specific
entities, be it General Motors, General Electric,
IBM, and others, the are finite in order. A
generalized statement would also be finite. Yet,
theoretical constructs, though remote from *immediate*
experience, are not entirely devoid of empirical
connotations. Carl G. Hempel in his powerful writing,
Fundamentals of Concept Formation in Empirical Science,
presented an excellent exposition of the relationship
between the theoretical plane and the observational
plane. He says:

> A scientific theory might therefore be likened to
> a complex spatial network: Its terms are repre-
> sented by the knots, while the threads connecting
> the latter correspond, in part, to the definitions
> and, in part, to the fundamental and derivative
> hypotheses included in the theory. The whole
> system floats, as it were, above the plane of
> observation and is anchored to it by rules of
> interpretation. These might be viewed as strings
> which are not part of the network but link certain
> points of the latter with specific places in the
> plane of observation. By virtue of those inter-
> pretive connections, the network can function as
> a scientific theory: From certain observational
> data, we may ascend, via an interpretive string,
> to some point in the theoretical network, thence
> proceed, via definitions and hypotheses, to
> other points, from which another interpretive
> string permits a descent to the plane of observa-
> tion.

In this manner an interpreted theory makes it possible to infer the occurrence of certain phenomena which can be described in observational terms and which may belong to the past or the future, on the basis of other such phenomena, whose occurrence has been previously ascertained. But the theoretical apparatus which provides these predictive and postdictive bridges from observational data to potential observational findings cannot, in general, be formulated in terms of observables alone. The entire history of scientific endeavor appears to show that in our world comprehensive, simple, and dependable principles for the explanation and prediction of observable phenomena cannot be obtained by merely summarizing and inductively generalizing observational findings. A hypothetico-deductive-observational procedure is called for and is indeed followed in the more advanced branches of empirical science: Guided by his knowledge of observational data, the scientist has to invent a set of concepts— theoretical constructs, which lack immediate experiential significance, a system of hypotheses couched in terms of them, and an interpretation for the resulting theoretical network; and all this is in a manner which will establish explanatory and predictive connections between the data of direct observation.[22]

[1]The year 1955 is more or less arbitrarily selected. Its selection, however, does have some relevance to the great debate on the structure of accounting theory between Professors A. C. Littleton and R. J. Chambers, ignited by the latter's "Blueprint for a Theory of Accounting," *Accounting Research* (January, 1955): pp. 17-25, which, I believe, has since rendered a tremendous impact upon accounting thinking.

[2]The two Latin phrases mean "before" and "after," respectively.

[3]It may be noted that David Hume referred to the analytic and synthetic as "relations of ideas" and "matters of fact." Alfred J. Ayer, for instance, in following Hume's vocabulary labeled the former a priori and the latter, hypothetical or empirical. See Ayer's *Language, Truth and Logic* (New York: Dover Publications, Inc., n.d.), p. 31.

[4]Neal W. Klausner and Paul G. Kuntz, *Philosophy: The Study of Alternative Beliefs* (The Macmillan Company, 1961), p. 212.

[5]Ludwig von Mises, *The Ultimate Foundation of Economic Science: An Essay on Methods* (D. Van Nostrand Company, Inc., 1962), p. 6.

[6]John G. Kemeny, *A Philosopher Looks at Science* (D. Van Nostrand Company, Inc., 1959), p. 22.

[7]A. C. Ewing, *The Fundamental Questions of Philosophy* (London: Routledge & Kegan Paul, 1951), p. 33.

[8]Ayer, op. cit., p. 137.

[9]Even if we confine ourselves to the study of
certain aspects of the total environment, it may still
be too complex for us to manage. An example given by
George J. Stigler relating to the study of economics
may be cited to illustrate this point. He says:
"Imagine a three dimensional jigsaw puzzle, consisting
of 100 million parts. Some parts touch against, let
us say, 1,000 other parts....Other parts touch, let us
be conservative, 50,000 other parts...but the real
difficulties have yet to be mentioned. The pieces
change shape quite often.... Meanwhile a busy set of
people...are changing rules.... And of course there are
other jigsaw puzzles of comparable complexity and
these other puzzles...are connected at literally a
million points with our puzzle." George J. Stigler,
The Theory of Price (The Macmillan Company, 3rd
edition, 1966), p. 7.

[10]The following exposition on definition is largely
based on Carl G. Hempel, *Fundamentals of Concepts
Formation in Empirical Science* (University of Chicago
Press, 1952); Morris R. Cohen and Ernest Nagel, An
Introduction to Logic and Scientific Method (Harcourt,
Brace & World, Inc., 1934); Richard Robinson,
Definition (Clarendon Press, Oxford, 1950); Rudolf
Carnap, *The Logical Syntax of Language* (London:
Kegan Paul, Trench, Trubner & Co. Ltd., 1937); and
_____, *Foundations of Logic and Mathematics*
(University of Chicago Press, 1960). Readers may
also refer to some other prominent writings on logic
and philosophy of science since almost all of them have
references to meanings of words and signs, together
with their relevance to the formation and explication
of constructs.

[11]Plato, *Euthyphro, Apology, and Crito,* F. J.
Church, tr., Robert D. Cummings, reviser (New York:
The Liberal Arts Press, 1948).

[12]Hempel, op. cit., p. 9.

[13]P. W. Bridgman, "Operational Analysis," *Philosophy of Science,* V (Appleton-Century-Crofts, 1938), p. 119.

[14]Peter Caws, "Definition and Measurement in Physics," *Measurement:Definitions, and Theories,* ed. C. West Churchman and Philburn Ratoosh (New York: John Wiley & Sons, Inc., 1959), p. 3.

[15]Kermit D. Larson, "Implications of Measurement Theory of Accounting Concept Formulation," *The Accounting Review,* January, 1969, p. 40.

[16]Ibid., p. 41. See also Henry Margenau, "What is a Theory?" *The Structure of Economic Science,* ed. S. R. Krupp (Englewood Cliffs: Prentice-Hall, 1966), p. 33.

[17]Larson, Ibid., pp. 41-42.

[18]Rudolf Carnap, *Logical Foundation of Probability* (Chicago: The University of Chicago Press, 1962), p. 3.

[19]Ibid., p. 5.

[20]P. W. Bridgman, *The Logic of Modern Physics* (New York: The Macmillan Company, 1927), pp. 28, 31 and 53.

[21]Fritz Machlup, "Operationalism and Pure Theory in Economics" *The Structure of Economic Science,* ed. S. R. Krupp (Prentice-Hall, 1966), pp. 56-57.

[22]Hempel, op. cit., pp. 36-37.

5 Normative and Positive Modes of Accounting Thought

The search for a theoretical framework of accounting during the past several decades has resulted in a variety of accounting thought, a variety which may be broadly divided into two major schools—normative and positive. The normative school is founded largely on a number of ethical and welfare concepts and places emphasis on value statements, issues relating to goal-determination and user needs, and interpretation of accounting information. The positive school of thought, in general, views accounting as a branch of systematized learning in terms of logical rigor and empirical correspondence, with emphasis on the neutrality of depicting and reporting accounting events. Between these two extremes, there are mixtures of both views with varying degrees of emphasis on one or the other.

The major purpose of this chapter is to present
a critical examination of the positive and normative
modes of accounting thought, with particular reference
to their epistemological foundations and empirical
validity. Specifically, we intend to investigate
the following questions. What are the nature and
meaning of normative, ethical statements? What are
some of the basic modes of normative and positive
accounting thought? Are positive and normative statements compatible within a discipline? Is accounting
such a discipline that there is room for both types
of statements? Is there a sequence by which one type
of statement precedes the other in theory construction?

Although there may not be ready answers to these
questions, it is hoped that a discourse on the normative
and positive phases of accounting will at least provide
a better understanding of the basic nature and function
of the accounting discipline and, perhaps, will also
stimulate some constructive thinking toward it. We
may take some small comfort here in the realization
that the positive versus normative controversy is not
at all peculiar to accounting. Some mature disciplines,
relatively speaking, such as economics, have been
troubled for years by the value issue. Some
economists contend, for instance, that welfare
economics is not a science, but an art; others maintain
that interpretation and application of economic theories
are outside the sphere of positive economics. While
the "value" controversy in economics is far from being
resolved, accounting in this respect is in a much
more confused situation, since accounting at present

does not even have a positive frame of reference.
The kind of accounting that we practice is largely
founded on a normative basis. An introduction of
a *positive* approach to theory formation in accounting
will undoubtedly present a serious threat to the
traditionally value-oriented accounting. We have
often heard that by nature accounting ought to be
a normative discipline. Unless we can satisfy the
question, "Why ought it to be so," however, such
an assertion must be held as an authoritative or
opinionated statement which, in a scientific sense,
cannot blindly be accepted.

Normative Accounting

The Basic Nature and Meaning of Normative Statements
——   Besides analytic and synthetic propositions as
expounded in the preceding chapter, there is a type
of statement the validity or truth values of which
may or may not be established through an analysis
of the meaning of the words used or by empirical
verification. These statements are known as value,
ethical, or normative assertions, and often contain
some imperative, commanding, wishful, or judgmental
words, such as "ought" or "ought not," "good" or
"bad," "right" or "wrong," "beautiful" or "ugly,"
"fair" or "unfair," and so forth. It has been said
that what is commanded, wished, or judged makes no
commitment as to truth or falsity. Philosophers
since ancient times have speculated upon the nature
and meaning of value assertions and have advanced
many modes of thought, ranging from metaphysics to
modern empiricism. The core of ethical philosophy

(a subdivision of axiology—the study of the general
theory of values) is concerned with the nature and
criteria of the "good," and extends to the "ought"
versus the "is." Some of the basic problems of
ethical philosophy include the origin or derivation
of the good, the absoluteness or relativeness of
the good, its deterministic or indeterministic nature,
the development of ethical standards for guiding
and judging good (or bad) conduct, and the epistemological
validity of ethical, normative assertions. The
intricate nature of ethical concepts has bewildered
even some of the most able thinkers in human history.
The following summary and remarks are based on a
sample of eight selected views of ethical or moral
philosophy: (1) ethical thought of Greek philosophers,
(2) Spinozistic determinism, (3) formalism,
(4) utilitarianism, (5) evolutionism, (6) pragmatism,
(7) instrumentalism, and (8) logical positivism.[2]
These selected views reveal significant differences
among one another. At the expense of oversimplification,
they are grouped and recapitulated as follows:
(1) the highest good resides with the ultimate reality
and can be studied only in a metaphysical context;
(2) moral issues, like all other things in the universe,
are determined by the infinite mind and hence are
neutral to us—another metaphysical viewpoint;
(3) from an evolutionistic viewpoint, "good" is
synonymous with the evolution of nature; (4) from a
rationalistic viewpoint, ethical concepts and
principles are a priori; (5) from one of the
empiricist viewpoints, normative ethical statements

are a posteriori;and (6) from a positivistic
viewpoint, normative ethical assertions are not
subject to analysis—logically or empirically—and
hence are meaningless.

An issue relating directly to value judgments
is the controversy of the "is" and the "ought"
statements. The debate among moral philosophers in
this connection is often centered around the choice
between holding that "ought" statements can be
based on "is" statements and contending that, as
defended by Immanuel Kant, "ought" statements are
independent and autonomous. Modern empiricists,
however, contend that a statement which takes the
commanding, imperative, or authoritative form
either has no factual content or is not subject to
logical analysis. Further, they insist that an
"ought" conclusion cannot be made out of an "is"
premise. David Hume forewarned of this, and
affirmed that one could not leap from a proposition
with the copula "is" to a proposition with the
copula "ought."[3] An imperative is not objective
and, not being objective, becomes subjective.
Further, an imperative often has a future referent,
and this very referent rules out any factual
correspondence. Thus, to the logical empiricist,
it is fruitless to try to settle normative, ethical
assertions on any logical or empirical grounds.

With the exception of logical positivism, each
of these ethical systems attempts to find a firm
foundation for ethical statements. The several
modes of ethical philosophy, however, reveal no
universal agreement as to how ethical concepts

and principles are founded and derived. It appears
that the most one can say about normative ethical
assertions is that there is a pluralism of ethical
theories or that we have not yet succeeded in
finding a general comprehensive theory of ethics.

The Several Modes of Normative Accounting Thought

—— The foregoing discussion on the epistemological
conditions of knowledge is intended to serve as a
guide to a critical examination of the normative
school of accounting thought, which, as compared with
the positive school, has been by far the predominant
one. In brief, we hold in theorization (a process
of shaping thought or belief), that whatever is
expressed must be capable of being affirmed,
demonstrated, doubted, or denied. Since accounting
is by nature an empirical discipline, examination
of normative accounting assertions will be made
not merely in terms of their logical rigor, but
also in terms of their empirical correspondence.
Five modes of normative accounting thought are
identified in this chapter: (1) ethical accounting,
(2) social welfare accounting, (3) user-oriented
accounting, (4) normative deductivism, and (5) the
goal-determination issue. It may be noted that
these modes overlap one another in varying degree
and that a clear distinction between them is not
always possible.

Ethical Accounting. Probably the most prominent mode
of normative thought in accounting is the "fairness"
doctrine which, together with the concepts of "justice,"

"equity," and "truth," constitutes the basic core
of what we call "ethical approach."[4] DR Scott has
been given general credit for the significant,
lasting impact of ethical concepts on accounting.
Scott asserts that the social concepts of fairness,
justice, and truth underlie all social organizations
and that, as such, they form the basis upon which
accounting principles and practice rest.[5] He
aligns "justice" with *equitable* treatment of all
interested parties, "truth" to *true* and *accurate*
accounting, and "fairness" to *fair*, *unbiased*, and
impartial presentation. Equating truth with a
scientific or objective connotation, Scott contends
that the truth concept eventually will replace
justice and fairness and, hence, will become the
transcendent "principle" of accounting.[6] Accountants
since Scott have, in general, regarded these three
concepts as implied within one another or as
equivalent or synonymous concepts. A clear-cut
distinction among the three is not evident in the
accounting literature. Most interpretations tend
to be circular. Upon closer examination, however,
it appears that, while justice and fairness may be
characterized as ethical norms, the truth concept
is more than a value statement; that is, it may
have, as implied by Scott, a "truth-value." Of
particular importance is that through the years,
ethical accountants have placed the emphasis
primarily on the "fairness" concept; however, we
are not certain as to the precise meaning of this
seemingly crucial accounting concept. At one

extreme, fairness has been visualized as a *self-evident* ethical norm not subject to proof or dispute. At the other extreme, it has been identified with impartiality or objectivity. In any event, the basic question still remains: What is fair? The primary difficulty of expounding and applying the fairness concept lies in the fact that it is by nature a value assertion. When we say that fairness means fair presentation in terms of *good faith*, plus *good* business practice, plus *good* accounting *judgment*, we are merely substituting one value statement for another.[7]

The ambiguity of the fairness concept (if it is a concept at all) is more than one normally comprehends in the sense that it has been variously applied in accounting. For instance, James W. Pattillo in his highly value-oriented writing, *The Foundation of Financial Accounting*, treated "fairness" as "a basic *standard* by which all subordinate propositions [of accounting] are judged."[8] He took issue with two of Scott's social concepts—justice and truth. To Pattillo, justice was "...a too rigid adherence to 'what is right and proper.'"[9] As to "truth," he held that absolute truth was an unattainable ideal. Only relative truth might be approached and, as such, the concept of truth must be subordinated to other considerations. Pattillo maintained therefore that "fairness," as applied to accounting, emerged as the choice over the other concepts (such as justice, equity, impartiality, unbiasedness, and objectivity) mainly on the ground that it implied

"ethical considerations."[10] Leonard Spacek went
so far as to claim that fairness was not only *the*
basic postulate of accounting upon which all aspects
of accounting rested but, most of all, "fairness of
accounting and reporting must be for and to
people...."[11] While accepting fairness as a basic
concept, Paul Grady preferred to treat fairness
in terms of "fair presentation" as the broad
objective of financial statements.[12] In *Statement
of the Accounting Principles Board No. 4* the Board
viewed "fair presentation" as the qualitative
standard of generally accepted accounting principles.[13]

Whatever "fairness" may connote, it has been
such an influential mode of normative thinking in
accounting through the years as to have shaped
the status of conventional accounting as we know
it today. Upon a closer examination, we see that
fairness under conventional accounting has another
significant dimension—we are referring to the
phrase, "present fairly," in the auditor's standard
short form report. The Committee on Auditing Procedure
of the American Institute of CPA's refers to the
following as the criteria for fair presentation:
(1) conformity with generally accepted accounting
principles (GAAP), (2) disclosure, (3) consistency,
and (4) comparability.[14] Notice the redundancy of
the Committee's items (2), (3), and (4) because
they are also GAAP. In an unqualified report, the
auditior is required to state not only the manner
in which the audit was conducted (i.e., in accordance
with generally accepted auditing standards— GAAS)

and the conditions under which the accompanying
financial statements were prepared (i.e., in
conformity with generally accepted accounting
principles applied on a consistent basis), but also
to express his opinion under the phrase "present
fairly." If compliance with GAAS and GAAP is
sufficient to render an unqualified opinion, then
the wording "present fairly" obviously becomes
redundant, but this does not seem to be the situation.
The inclusion of the phrase is clearly intended to
reflect the auditor's *judgment*. It may be that a
judgment of this sort, reflecting an expert or
professional opinion, is psychologically desirable
in the sense that it will increase the confidence
of financial statement users. In any event, there
exist double standards, with the first standard
(i.e., compliance with GAAS and GAAP) subject to
the second one (i.e., the auditor's value judgment).
Thus it is quite possible that in some circumstances
the auditor could qualify his opinion, despite the
fact that the accompanying financial statements
were prepared in conformity with GAAP and the audit
was conducted in accordance with GAAS. As pointed
out by William W. Werntz, we are, in essence,
allowing the auditor to substitute "...for the test
of generally accepted accounting principles an
undefined and subjective concept of 'fairness.'"[15]

Given this value concept, there exists the
qualitative problem of "fairness." Why merely "fair"?
How about "fairer" or even "fairest"?[16] In
addition, it appears that the auditor's "fairness"

opinion is often mixed with management's favoritism, for given accepted alternative accounting principles, management will naturally select those which give the most favorable picture of the firm's performance.

Epistemologically, it is difficult to categorize the "fairness" assertion. If the nature of fairness rests with ultimate reality or truth, it must be examined in a metaphysical context. If fairness could be known by reason only, then the rationalistic mode of thought to substain its validity would prevail. As such, it would be treated as a priori. Under empiricism, there are two possibilities. One would be that the fairness concept might have an empirical correspondence and that its validity could be established through observation of a given society's value system. The other would be to treat it as a normative, ethical notion which would have no logical or factual content.

The basic strength of the ethical mode of accounting thought lies in the seemingly simple, self-evident "fairness" concept. Being fair is virtuous and it is socially unacceptable to speak against, or even doubt, any idea that is virtuous. In theory construction, however, it is necessary to substantiate, logically or empirically, whatever is asserted. For a discipline which is operational in nature, one must specify the operational capacities of its basic concepts, for failing to meet this fundamental requirement will almost always cause its subsequent operations to be in a state of confusion and ambiguity, especially in measurement terms. A broad concept, when taken in toto, is often constitutive in nature, and it is the researcher's task, whenever possible, to make it operational by identifying its operational properties or by setting forth certain specifications under which it plays its assigned role in the discipline. Thus, it is fruitless to use judgmental terms to preach how important fairness is to accounting. On the other hand, when its operational capacity, if any, is determined through a process of concept explication, which in turn is enforced by sufficient empirical research, then and only then, would it be possible either to define fairness in measurement terms or to use it as a qualitative concept governed by a set of specific operational standards. Under the first possibility, fairness would become an operational concept in its own right; under the second possibility, it could be made operational by surrogation.

Social Welfare Accounting. The ethical approach discussed in the preceding section centers primarily around a single value concept—fairness. There is another mode of normative accounting thought which, with variants, has a much wider ethical view and has a utilitarian theme. In general, this pattern of normative accounting thought appeals to certain allegedly "established social values." These social values are referred to as guiding criteria for the determination of basic objectives of accounting in terms of equity and usefulness of accounting data in serving the various interests of society. Instead

of relying on some a priori value notions, the
"social-value oriented" accountant believes that a
careful observation of the socioeconomic environment
will reveal a set of established social values, and
it is this social value system which basically
determines the goals of accounting and shapes of
the content of accounting information.

The belief that accounting serves a useful
social purpose is not entirely new. Examination of
accounting literature—traditional and contemporary
—yields an abundance of writings holding this view.
The beginning section of *Accounting Research Bulletin
No. 1*, published in 1939, bears the heading "Accounting
and the Social System," and states that "...Broadly
speaking, it [corporate accounting] will serve a
useful social purpose. The test of the corporate
system and of the special phase of it represented
by corporate accounting ultimately lies in the results
which are produced. These results must be judged
from the standpoint of society as a whole—not from
that of any one group of interested parties."[17]

William A. Paton and A. C. Littleton in their
An Introduction to Corporate Accounting Standards
contend that large corporations are quasi-public
institutions which have a duty to the general public
interests (including those of investors, wage
earners, consumers, and the government), that the
public interests of corporations call for recognition
by corporate management of public responsibilities,
and that resources should be allocated to those
industries which serve the public interests.[18]

A similar assertion that accounting has an obligation
to serve the public interests in terms of effective
allocation and utilization of economic resources is
made by Littleton and V. K. Zimmerman in their
Accounting Theory: Continuity and Change.[19] A
Study Group at the University of Illinois considered
that maximization of the benefits of resource
utilization was important to all members of the society
and that the role of accounting was to provide information as a basis for effective evaluation of
management's stewardship and utilization of the society's
scarce means.[20] Professor E. Joe Demaris argues that
accounting contributions to the general welfare of the
society in terms of income reporting should be ranked
in a hierarchy of social importance.[21] In his book
on income theory, Norton Bedford claims that the
acquisition of income is the basic motivating force
directing human activity and that the social well-being
is maximized through a measure of income determination
that is *best* for the society. Accordingly, business
income determination will need social guidance or
justification.[22] In connection with operational
measurement of income, Bedford contends that the
amount measured "plays the role of a lubricant,
facilitating the functioning of society in an operational
sense. Specifically, measured income is used as a
computed amount to accomplish objectives necessary
for the operation of society."[23] The 1966 statement
of the American Accounting Association also carried
a social-welfare tone, stating that accounting should
develop the kind of information that would meet

individuals' needs as well as social wants.[24]   Yuji
Ijiri used the term "equity accounting" (as distinguishe
from "operational accounting") to signify the need
for a valuation system in terms of society's goals to
regulate conflicting interests.[25]

While emphasizing deductive reasoning in theory
formation, Carl Devine considered the necessity of
adopting "the accepted social standard" in order to
preserve equity in accounting operation. To Devine,
this would require a statement of accounting objectives
for guiding research in accounting. Although he
shared Alfred Jules Ayer's view on normative, ethical
statements, Devine appealed for the acceptance of an
existing social value system as a basis upon which
accounting goals rested.[26]   In a later writing, Devine
considered use of the social-value criterion as the
beginning step in designing measurement rules by
specifying and ordering the relative worth of different
objectives pursued by different interested groups.[27]

In following Devine's idea that a statement of
accounting objectives based on accepted social values
was the initial step in formulating a theoretical
framework of accounting, Alfred Rappaport attempted to
ascertain the objectives of corporate accounting
reports in terms of a "social consensus" concept.
After identifying five basic social values (briefly,
freedom via judicious restraint, political pluralism,
consent as a source of power, compromise, and economic
progress), Rappaport set forth four objectives of
corporate reports or "value-prescribed recommendations":
(1) a reporting obligation of managements, (2)
information essential to arriving at rational judgments,

(3) information promoting efficient allocation of
resources, and (4) information influencing socially
desirable behavior and discouraging undesirable
behavior. Like Devine, Rappaport, by appealing to
Ayer's distinction between "descriptive" and
"normative" ethical symbols, held that his value
statements were "descriptive ethical symbols rather
than normative symbols."[28]   Both Devine and Rappaport
maintained that a search of the social environment
would produce an established social value system.

Perhaps the most ambitious social-value oriented
accounting is the so-called socioeconomic accounting.[29]
It carries not only a social viewpoint but also a
political overtone. The emphasis is placed on social
and political consequences, as well as on economic
effects, of whatever activities of concern to
accounting. It is contended that society demands
responsible behavior in terms of social well-being.
Thus, the emphasis on economic consequences under
"traditional" accounting—including all the branches
of microaccounting and macroaccounting—is inadequate,
as it "neglects the social effects."[30]   Accounting,
as it goes, should provide the kind of information
for ranking and evaluating priorities of utilizing
resources in light of the overall objectives of a
given society. Thus, "maximization" must be extended
beyond the enterprise level, so that total social and
psychological satisfaction is increased. Activities
of business enterprises must be socially responsible
and the market orientation of business must be
extended to, or replaced by, the "human concept."
In other words, socioeconomic accounting places

emphasis on "social measurement." This seems to mean that the market criterion used for allocation of national resources is to be implemented by the "social-welfare criterion." In general, it is expected that under socioeconomic accounting accountants are to assume the kind of social responsibilities shared by economists, sociologists, statisticians, politicians, and government agencies.

Whether resting upon a single value concept or upon multiple ones, the value content of the "social well-being" mode of accounting thought, axiologically speaking, is just as great as that of conventional accounting. Initially, these social values must somehow be operationally defined or surrogated so that they can be functionally related to accounting theory and practice. Further, the asserted distinction between "descriptive" and "normative" symbols must await substantiation from extensive empirical research. In any event, the "social-welfare" issue is much broader than the present scope of the accounting discipline. In the first place, we will face the initial problems of ascertaining, in toto, the established social value structure, and of selecting those social values which accounting can fulfill and promote. In the second place, there exists the formidable value judgment problem of ordering those social values. The hope for successful implementation of this mode of accounting thought in theory constructic will probably rest, among other things, upon our ability to appeal to sociology, social psychology, political science, law, and welfare economics.

User-Oriented Accounting. The notion of social
well-being, particularly that of social equity, has
been advanced, in part, to the development of a much
narrower viewpoint in accounting—user needs, a very
popular mode of accounting thinking that has influenced the direction and content of accounting
research noticeably in recent years. An example
of this approach is the 1966 statement of the
American Accounting Association.[31] In general,
the user theory starts with the traditional notion
of equitable treatment of all interested parties,
extends to meeting specific user needs, and ends with
the usefulness of accounting information to society
as a whole. The content of the user theory is rather
complicated, ranging from identifying users and their
needs, specifying and modeling the information requirements of these identified users of accounting information, and designing information systems to postulating that social welfare is increased through
efficient allocation and utilization of scarce
resources at the private level, partly because of
the usefulness of accounting information.

We certainly have no quarrel with the contention
that user needs should govern and shape the content
of accounting information. What is at issue is
that we must somehow find satisfactory answers to
the following questions: Who are the users? How
do we determine their needs? How, and to what
extent, can we satisfy their specific needs, and hence
affect their, behavior—in a rational way, of course?

For internal users, we can take pride indeed in the
development of information systems and decision-model
building in accounting during the past decade or so.
Unfortunately, the same cannot be said about our
progress in external reporting; it is in this segment
of accounting that the validity and meaningfulness
of accounting information has been severely challenged.
External users consist of a large number of groups
of users with diversified needs. Since the interests
of users within each group may differ, it is conceivabl
that subdivisions of each group are necessary. Further
with conflicting interests among users, it means that,
when carried to the extreme, eventually accounting
outputs might have to be tailored to the decision
models of individual users. It may be noted that
even the same user may have a variety of needs for
accounting information.

   With respect to whether user needs are known
or knowable, one may, of course, either postulate
their diversified needs, followed by empirical
verification, or conduct extensive empirical reseach
to find out first hand their specific needs. These
are, to say the least, no small tasks. The real
problems, however, have yet to be mentioned; that is,
after users and their needs are identified, there
will come the formidable job of meeting their
diversified needs due to conceptual, technical, and
cost constraints.[32] Initially, one may have to limit
users to a small number of groups with emphasis on
their common needs. Even operating on such a limited
scale, however, the accountant would have to deal
directly with the identified users in order to, for

instance, specify and model the information requirements. What has been said should not be interpreted
as presenting an impossible situation. We have merely
tried to point out some of the serious problems
involved in the implementation of information systems
for external users. It is, of course, possible that
eventually there might be data bases in all industries
for use in designing specific information systems
for a limited number of users so that they would
have as privileged information as the internal users.

   Alternatively, we may raise the following
question: Why are we concerned with specific user
needs? Certainly, without users there would be no
reason or meaning for the existence of the accounting
discipline, except perhaps for the sake of the
accountant's own curiosity, but we need not be bothered
with a question of this sort. The users of accounting
information are not really interested in accounting
per se, but are actually interested in the occurrence
of a certain class of economic phenomena. With or
without accounting, this class of events takes place.
As long as accounting depicts, with necessary
constraints, the defined events in a neutral manner,
users decide their own needs and use the information
as they see fit. In other words, under this
alternative approach, the accountant provides users
with a data bank in the light of a valid theoretical
framework. The professional accountant may, of course,
perform the filtering, tailoring, or interpretative
function upon request *only* after he has fulfilled
his role as a fact finder or measurer.

The Efficient Market Hypothesis (EMH)   An
encouraging sign of empirical research in accounting
with respect to user's needs and behavior in recent
years is the enthused interest and efforts demonstrated
by a number of empirically oriented accountants in
testing the "efficient market hypothesis" for the purpo
of measuring and evaluating the potential content of
accounting information.[33]   The hypothesis takes the
following mathematical formulation known as the
expected returns model:[34]

$$Z_i, t+1 = r_i, t+1 - E[r_i, t+1 | \phi t]$$
and
$$E[Z_i, t+1 | \phi t] = 0$$

where $Z_i, t+1$ denotes the excess return for security
i in period $t+1$—the difference between the observed
return $r_i, t+1$ and the expected return given informatio
at ϕt.   Briefly, the underlying assumption of the
EMH is that security market prices reflect fully all
publicly available information and react instantaneous.
systematically, and without bias to new information.
Thus, "efficiency" of the stock market may be defined
as "the speed with which equilibrium is reached
after the release of some set of data."[35]   Fama
suggests three levels of market efficiency: weak,
semistrong, and strong.[36]   Market reactions to
accounting numbers, therefore, should govern
evaluations of the content of accounting information
and ultimately evaluations of the accounting procedure
used to produce these numbers.   In other words, the
EMH should prove whether accounting numbers (e.g.,
earnings per share) have informational content.

The semistrong form is of particular interst to
accountants because the information set contains
financial reports. Incidentally, the weak form
says that the market equilibrium reflects the
result of historical prices and the strong form
implements inside information.

With respect to testing the potential content
of accounting information, the EMH is not at all
frictionless and so far has been a controversial
issue.[37] First, the EMH seems more or less to
imply the economic model of perfect competition,
that is, the market through all the transactors
avails itself fully of all publicly available
information, resulting, in essence, in a fully
informed market (i.e., transactors may make mistakes
but they are not ignorant). Secondly, efficiency
is a property of the market, not of accounting
signals.[38] Without testing accounting measures
produced under alternative procedures, we cannot
say that they are the best measures generated under
existing accounting rules or that there are no
better measures. "People may react to a sign which
we call a 'lie.'"[39] There is a difference between
market equilibrium and optimality;[40] the former is
the result of readjusted demand and supply forces
due to new information, and the latter has something
to do with the quality of information. Thirdly,
users of accounting information may be so conditioned
that they react to accounting numbers at their
face value without questioning their validity or
meaningfulness. Fourthly, accounting is only a
part of the general information system and the extent

of the impact of accounting information upon the
market is empirically difficult to isolate. Fifthly,
the EMH deals with the aggregate behavior of transactors, not their individual behavior. This brings
out the issue of "homogeneous expectations" of the
market as a whole versus "heterogeneity of individual
expectations." From an accounting viewpoint, this
is an important issue, because reactions of individual
users to accounting information are some of the
most crucial issues in accounting today. This may
mean that accounting information may have more
dimensions than implied by the EMH. Sixthly, the
results of a number of empirical studies are not
consistent with the EMH. This does not mean that
we reject the hypothesis; rather, it means that the
empirical research on the EMH to date is not conclusive,
that more extensive empirical studies are needed,
and that a reexamination (or refinement) of the EMH
may be necessary (e.g., Downes and Dyckman contend
that the EMH using only an expected returns model
is too narrow and leads to the problems of
"decomposition.") We wish to note again that empirical
research is time consuming, requiring not only a
large number of performances but also controlled
and reproducible conditions and that the operating
properties and capacity of the model being tested
must be precisely defined. Finally, the EMH has
been tested so far by using only data from the
commodity markets and the American and New York
Stock Exchanges. Whether the content of accounting
information needs to be the same for less familiar

markets is a question for which we do not have an answer yet.[41]

Normative Deductivism. With few exceptions, the development of accounting theory in terms of orientation and research methodology since the 1950's may be characterized as following a normative mode of thinking in a deductive frame. In general, the normative deductivist starts his inquiry by including some allegedly universal value statements (e.g., fairness and usefulness), either in his predetermined objectives of accounting or in a set of basic postulates and concepts from which other propositions are deduced. Upon what grounds these value statements are established is not always clear. Most of the normative-deductive accountants often evade the label "ethical approach." Instead, they prefer to describe their approach as "postulational," "problem-oriented," "authoritative," "pragmatical," or simply "deductive." In addition, the writers of this school, in general, tend to confine their arguments within the world of accounting literature, resulting in a circular type of exposition.

As pointed out by Stephen Zeff, the conflict between the normative-deductive school of thought and the "positive-empirical" approach in accounting parallels neither the centuries-old debate among philosophers of science on rationalism versus empiricism nor the methodological dispute in economics among Milton Friedman, Fritz Machlup,

and Paul Samuelson.[42] The feud in accounting is
primarily an issue of ethical or value-oriented
accounting versus a scientific or positivistic
theory of accounting. Thus the issue at stake
here is more than the dispute over the basic nature
and meaning of accounting propositions—a priori
propositions versus a posteriori propositions or
deductivism versus inductivism.

A foremost critic of the normative-deductive
approach is Louis Goldberg who believes that
accounting principles are necessarily derived
from observation and generalization.[43] Goldberg's
empiricism calls for factual content in accounting
theory. The role of accounting is determined in the
actual environment, not by what accountants say
in their own circle. To Goldberg, what the normative-
deductive accountant is doing is essentially influencing
the behavior of users of accounting information in
accordance with the accountant's value judgments and
preferences. Goldberg contends that the accountant
is not capable of making the decision for users as
to what information they are supposed to have. In
discussing Goldberg's positive-empirical approach to
accounting theory, Zeff added that the emphasis on
user needs and the "pressure upon accounting researchers
to invent better information systems to feed the
insatiable appetite of sophisticated decision models
have almost eclipsed the concern for accumulating
knowledge, qua knowledge, about our field of study."[44]

The Goal-Determination Issue. The discussion of

normative accounting would be incomplete without a
word about the issue of goal determination. It has
frequently been contended that the search for a theoretical framework of accounting should begin with a
statement of precisely and explicitly defined accounting goals. The inevitable questions are: What are
the goals of accounting and how are they determined?

Accountants have defined accounting goals in
such a variety of ways that there exists no general
agreement among them on this seemingly crucial issue.
In addition, there are often competing and conflicting
ends which must somehow be reconciled and ranked.
We believe that at this point it will be very helpful
to differentiate goals or ends from means. In general,
means are instruments or devices reflecting our
acquaintance with certain ways of doing things.
Often there are alternative means for achieving a
given end. The determination of a particular goal
and the selection of a suitable means to achieve
the specified or desired end are matters of decision
making involving choice among alternatives. The whole
situation can best be described by the following
statements: "What it ought to be," and "what we
ought to do."

As previously discussed, it is, to say the
least, not a simple matter to establish, logically
or empirically, the truth-value of an "ought"
statement. Because of this, the scientist in general
regards "ought" statements, together with value
assertions, as outside the realm of scientific
inquiry. John G. Kemeny, noted philosopher of
science and a mathematician, warns that "scientific

statements in themselves cannot serve as a source
of value judgments."[45] The implication is that
value statements cannot be deduced directly from
either analytic or synthetic statements. Although
the scientist is no better equipped than anyone
else to decide upon value issues, he is the one
whom we can consult for means. Suppose we have
decided that pollution must be stopped. We do not
and cannot at this stage determine among ourselves
how to go about attaining this *desired* goal.
Rather, we go to the scientists who know, or are
supposed to know, the means available for achieving
it. Although the scientist does not make the choice
for us, he does provide a valuable service, in
addition to indicating what means are available.
He can tell us the different consequences of the
available means and thus give us some idea about
the future result of whatever decision we may make.
The scientist seeks no agreement on value issues.
There is, of course, the danger of overlooking human
well-being, but this is a matter which must be
evaluated outside the domain of science, qua science.

One may contend that all activities are goal
oriented and that the activities of accounting are
necessarily associated with its goals. Upon closer
examination, however, we see that accounting activities
are, in essence, a part of those of a given entity
which, not of accounting, has definite goals. In
addition, the contention that accounting is the
language of business signifies, in part at least,
that accounting is a service discipline facilitating
business operations and that most accounting activities

are specified and required by management. Thus, it will be more accurate and meaningful to define the basic function of accounting than to determine its goals.

Probably the most we can say about the goal issue in accounting is that accounting produces relevant and meaningful information. But even this seemingly value-free statement is not a simple matter. It has been said that in the measurement process, we identify and measure only the relevant properties of an object, provided they are measurable. How do we identify the *relevant* properties? We admit that it is in part the theorist's privilege to decide what are relevant and what are irrelevant. So an element of value judgment on the part of the theorist is involved. The question again is: To what extent do we wish to carry out value judgments in the search of a theoretical framework?

The goal issue is no small matter and has caused endless debates in accounting. With diversified opinions on accounting goals, it is only natural to have diversified opinions on the content of accounting theory. It is true that a discipline usually can accommodate a number of theories, compatible or incompatible. If the situation is created by value assertions without logical or empirical support, however, it will defy the very hope of finding a formal structure for the discipline. The heart of the goal issue in accounting is that it is inherently a part of the normative phase of accounting operations (such as interpre-

tation and evaluation of accounting events as well
as the determination of usefulness of accounting
information); and we hold that it is detachable
from the structure of accounting theory proper.

Positive Accounting

The Nature and Meaning of Positive Accounting
—— A discipline which employs the *positive*
approach is said to be free of value issues, and
its theory structure is intended to be a basic
framework for explaining and predicting a class of
phenomena explicitly defined within the boundaries
of the discipline. The formulation of a positive
theory is to work out a coherent set of propositions
free of any value connotations, psychological factors,
or goal determination. Analysis of a factual
situation in the light of such a positive frame of
reference is entirely objective in the sense that
"anyone starting with the same data and using the
same rules of logic must arrive at the same
conclusions."[46] In a strict sense the domain of
science accepts only positive statements (logical
and empirical) and has no tolerance for value or
ethical assertions of any kind.

The preceding discussion presents the positive
approach in its purest form, that is, entirely free
of value symbols. As previously stated, value
judgment, however slight in magnitude, is probably
unavoidable in any kind of intellectual inquiry.
The attempt to remove completely all ethical and
psychological factors from scientific studies,
particularly in the area of the social sciences, is

unlikely to succeed. Accordingly, the formulation
of a positivistic system is necessarily on a relative
basis. What the scientist actually does is to
minimize, to the extent humanly possible, the weight
of normative symbols upon his analysis. For instance,
he may try first to purify his postulates, because
postulates infested with value symbols produce
value conclusions. The issue is not that value
judgments are entirely irrelevant in any scientific
discipline; rather it is the manner in which a
formal structure is constructed and the *timing*
when value judgments or interpretations enter the
picture. It is probably safe to say that in the
end a matured discipline will need both analytic
and interpretive statements but that the former is
necessarily the basis of the latter. This may
mean that judgmental assertions are detachable
from the theoretical structure proper. In theory
construction there are two crucial points susceptible
to value symbols: derivation of a set of basic
postulates free of value connotations and theory
verification free of intentional search for a
desirable end. The elegance of a positivistic
system lies in its logical coherence, as well as
empirical correspondence, but, most of all, in its
neutrality to unanalyzable and unverifiable value
statements. These powerful characteristics of
positivism make a formal structure possible.

Although it is not always easy to draw a
clear-cut demarcation of the positive and normative
phases of a discipline, we hold that it is

theoretically significant to separate, to the extent
possible, these two phases in any scientific study.
In general, the positive phase of a discipline is
concerned with logical and empirical analysis of a
given class of phenomena free of emotive connotations,
while its normative phase involves interpretation
of the results of the analysis in the form of
evaluation or decision recommendation.

The Positive School of Accounting Thought——A
leading figure taking a strong positivistic
or neutralistic position is R. J. Chambers. To
Chambers, the pursuit of knowledge is to enable
men to "adapt themselves to, or seek to mitigate
the effects of, their environment."[47] He holds
that accounting is a "process of discovering, of
getting the facts," and that as such accounting is
not different from other empirical sciences.[48]
The determination and ranking of "ends" are outside
the theory structure of Chambers, because such
actions necessarily require value judgments which
are not subject to verification except in an
ex post facto manner. Therefore, we must regard ends
as given and beyond inquiry.[49] Thus, Chambers
argues that accounting inquiry, "like that of
economics, is entirely neutral between ends."[50]
A basic theme of Chambers' theory is that the human
actor is viewed as an organism, which is regarded
as a "homeostatic system, constantly adapting itself
to its environment so that its capacity for
functioning, its survival, is assured."[51] The
preceding quoted statement reveals the means-end

relationship. Since ends are beyond inquiry,
however, the major concern of a discipline is
focused upon means. In other words, means is the
major concern of science. The main properties of
Chambers' "independence-of-means" thesis are
objectivity, relevance, neutrality, uniformity,
adaptability, and reliability.[52] Because of the
neutrality property, Chambers confutes the validity
of the so-called user theory of accounting.

In selecting a proper approach to the formulation
of a general theory of accounting, Maurice Moonitz
in his *Accounting Research Study No. 1 (ARS 1)*
rejects the ethical approach, the pragmatic approach,
the behavioral approach, and the axiomatic approach.
To Moonitz, normative concepts (i.e., justice,
truth, and fairness) are subjective assertions.
As to pragmatism, he identifies it with "usefulness,"
and raises the question: "Useful to whom? and
for what purpose?" Moonitz refuted the behavioral
approach on the ground that the researcher's own
behavior would interact with his research work.
Although he regarded the axiomatic approach as being
too abstract and incapable of dealing with the
empirical part of accounting, he hastily came to the
conclusion that "relatively heavy reliance must be
placed on deductive reasoning in the development
of accounting postulates and principles."[53]
Although the discussion on methodology presented
by Moonitz in ARS 1 is far from complete and
satisfactory, his intention to seek an objective,
neutral position in the development of a theoretical
framework of accounting is unmistakably clear.[54]

A position similar to those of Chambers and
Moonitz is taken by Harold E. Arnett. In addition
to emphasizing an "objective or scientific approach—
observation and deductive logic," Arnett criticized
the subjectivity of the ethical approach to
accounting theory formation on the ground that the
approach would direct our attention to the *interests*
of the accounting entity. To Arnett, the "entity"
should be the focal point of the accounting discipline.[5]
In a monograph entitled *Objectivity in Accounting,*
Curtis H. Stanley asserted that theory was created
by the mind and that the validity of a theory rested
upon its "deductive certainty." To Stanley, empirical
correspondence and the notions of fairness and usefulness
should not affect theory formation, although these
elements may be introduced at a later stage.[56] F. R.
Morgan viewed accounting as a "scientific method"
or a statistical tool of the business man; as such,
accounting had no theory of its own.[57] In an
ambitious attempt, Sewell Bray has tried to formulate
"a pure theory of accounting which seeks to apply
universal concepts of structure for, and measurement
to, any and every economic activity...."[58] William
L. Raby treated the accounting entity as an "economic
entity" which was real and must be dealt with in a
total manner (i.e., "something greater than a sum
of its parts....")[59] In distinguishing two ways
that the accountant would perform—reporting and
interpreting, Raby contended that the accountant
"should refrain from engaging in interpretation"
and must not be assailed by the temptation to censor

and interpret objectively derived accounting data.[60]

A fairly recent positivistic attempt at accounting theory which has received considerable attention is known as the "events approach." In his "An Events Approach to Basic Accounting Theory," George H. Sorter places emphasis on "events" rather than "values."[61] He challenges the validity of the "value theorist's" assertion about user needs. To Sorter, the value-oriented mode of accounting thinking is subjective and personal. "User needs" are unknown or unknowable. In reality, there is a variety of uses of accounting data, and "it is therefore impossible to specify input values that are optimal for the wide range of possible users...Neither economists nor accountants have been able to advance the theoretically correct decision models."[62] Both income determination and asset valuation call for a "value" position on the part of the accountant. In other words, the value accountant assigns specific weights to accounting information in order to have the data fit specific decision models. To Sorter, the users are entitled to "unweighted" raw data, and any weights and values suggested by the accountant should be communicated to the users in *disaggregated* form. "Proponents of the 'events' theory suggests that the purpose of accounting is to provide information about relevant economic events...[which] allows individual users to generate their own input values for their own individual decision models."[63]

Under the events approach, the balance sheet, the income statement, and the funds statement are

regarded as communicative devices reporting different
classes of events or activities. These statements
should not be viewed as reports on specific events
or as rationalization of particular costs or values.
Thus to the events theorist, asset values, income
values, and the magnitude of working capital are not
only restrictive measures but also are insignificant.
The essence of accounting information should consist
largely of relevant events, such as aggregate events,
operating events, and financial and investment events.
Sorter also takes issue with the American Accounting
Association's *Statement of Basic Accounting Theory*,
because of its emphasis on "user needs," which to
Sorter is a value-oriented approach.[64] In general,
Sorter's argument in terms of means and ends is
quite similar to that of Chambers and Moonitz. The
events system is far from being complete. In a
recent paper, Orace Johnson tries to make the events
approach operational in terms of identifying and
measuring relevant events.[65]

With emphasis on observations to determine
what accounting phenomena are, Louis Goldberg's
thought with respect to the essence of accounting
theory is quite akin to that of early empiricism.
In his article "Varieties of Accounting Theory,"
Goldberg distinguishes between "accounting
doctrine" (i.e., "theory sense 1") and "accounting
theory" (or "theory sense 2"), contending that
"doctrine" deals with "precepts" or what should be
and that theory is concerned with what *is*.[66] He
further classifies "theory sense 2" into "theory

sense 2-A" and "theory sense 2-B". Under theory
sense 2-A, it is up to us to find out what accounting
is through observation. This is followed by the
development of hypotheses which in turn will lead
to some kind of generalization. The emphasis is
placed on "observed and recorded data." In other
words, theory sense 2-A is largely descriptive
in nature. Theory sense 2-B is concerned with
explanatory and predictive capacity of a theory
substantiated again by observation and confirmation.
In general, Goldberg rejects a priori reasoning for
theory formation.[67]

Yuji Ijiri axiomized conventional accounting
in his *Foundations of Accounting Measurement*,[68]
but this did not make conventional accounting value
free or correspond with economic reality. In a
subsequent writing, however, he differentiates,
vigorously, three areas of accounting ("the triad
of accounting")——theories, policies, and practices—
and rightly contends that accounting theories should
be free of value judgment.[69] Accounting theories,
like those of other disciplines (such as linguistics,
meteorology, or chemistry), are derived from empirical
observations by means of abstraction. In the process
of observation, the scientist does not make "a
value judgment as to what the empirical phenomena
ought to be." The scientist's objective in building
theories "is to explain a huge volume of observations
by an organized set of concepts. Whether or not
these phenomena are desirable for the welfare of
human beings is irrelevant in the theory-building

process."[70]   Ijiri views accounting theorists as
scientific observers of accounting practices and
their surrounding environment.   In conclusion, he
says that it is the role of accounting policy makers,
not that of accounting theorists, to "define the
goals of the accounting profession, evaluate means
to achieve the goals, and implement them by
establishing accounting policies.   Value judgment
being a subjective operation, the role of policy
makers is subjective.   What they develop is an
opinion and not a theory,what it should be and not
what it is."[71]

*Summary and Conclusions—An Evaluation of the Two
Phases of the Accounting Discipline*

> It would be silly indeed to argue or quarrel
> about the height of a tree, the weight of a
> stone, or the distance of a mountain from a
> certain point.   The answer is never won in the
> triumph of a debate, but rather by the simple
> steps of measurement.   When men do dispute,
> it is frequently about some problem of moral
> issue.   Is this act proper, right, desirable,
> good?   Or is it improper, wrong, undesirable,
> evil?   Surround these questions with different
> points of view and you have the possibility
> of vigorous controversy. [72]

With the above quotation, let us recapitulate,
evaluate, and conclude what has been said about
normative accounting and positive accounting as well
as their relationships, if any.   As discussed in
the early part of this chapter, a discipline which
follows a positive approach is said to be free of
value issues, and its theory structure is intended
as a basic framework for analyzing, explaining,
and predicting a class of phenomena explicitly

defined within the boundaries of the discipline.
It will be a rare occasion, however, to employ
the positive approach in its purest form, that is,
completely free of value judgment. Even in a
scientific inquiry, the selection of a certain
object for study, the employment of proper methodology,
the derivation of a set of postulates, what is to be
observed, the pattern and number of tests to be
conducted, and so forth, necessarily involve a degree
of value judgment on the part of the researcher. In
other words, the researcher's privilege and decision
to do any of those things are already judgmental
matters. What the scientist actually attempts to
accomplish is to minimize, to the extent humanly
possible, the weight or impact of normative symbols
upon his work.

Turning to normative, ethical statements, we
see that philosophers through the centuries have
not been able to establish any common foundations
for value assertions. On top of all the various
modes of philosophical thought, there exists an
operational problem of value concepts, that is,
whether they can be operationally defined for measurement purposes. Basically this problem lies in the
realm of operationalism—a variant of modern empiricism.
If value concepts can be operationally defined, we
certainly would like to know what the measurement
rules, scales, and units of measure are. If value
concepts are not measurable in quantitative terms
but can be used as "norms" for guiding actions,
then we would like to have them empirically substantiated,

followed by establishing a set of operating rules, so that the employment of value concepts in accounting operations would not be so much a matter of preaching virtuous things, personal beliefs, opinions, or judgments. But these are no small orders, and attempts to establish the operational capacity of value concepts in other disciplines (particularly in the social sciences) have been so controversial and inconclusive as to make one wonder whether, methodologically speaking, we will succeed in this respect in the accounting discipline. In brief, value statements are much larger assertions than scientific propositions.

We wish to emphasize that what has been said about normative, ethical statements does not at all minimize their significance. Indeed, ethics has been a crucial subject ever since the dawn of human history. Many critical crises in history arose from conflicts in ethical issues. In our daily life, a day rarely passes without our exercising some kind of value judgment. With the scientific advancement during the past century, there is no doubt that ethical philosophy, increasingly, has become more crucial than ever before. Few, if any, would deny that technological progress has resulted in increased tension and conflicts in the social, ecnomic, and political life of man.

It has been said that value assertions are a necessity in the study of the relations among men and the interaction between men and their physical environment in terms of moral principles and criteria, social value system, desirable ends, and cultural ideology. On the other hand, the physical scientist would contend that the social sciences, because of their value orientation, are "psuedo science." Whether or not the social sciences are sciences, qua science, is of no particular importance to us. What concerns us most is how to establish the truth values and operating capacities of normative, ethical statements in theory construction, verification, and application. We wish to emphasize once again that in theory formation, one must, sooner or later, come to terms with the conditions of knowledge acquisiton. When the conditions of value statements cannot be established undisputedly in epistemological terms, we are on notice that such statements be accorded a different kind of treatment.

Given the value issue, many misconceptions exist about normative statements, especially in the social sciences. The misconceptions are caused largely by a mix-up of positive elements and value elements in theorization; the philosopher of science has told us repeatedly that they are eminently distinct. As a human being, the scientist often plays dual roles—the finder or measurer and the interpreter or appraiser. The finder role must come first. As to the appraiser role, it requires, among other things, opinions and judgments. The danger is, of course, that when the scientist fails to separate these double roles, he will carry an emotive tone into his work, or will attempt to exercise value judgments

toward finding desirable ends or results. This is
more likely to happen in the social sciences, largely
because the social sciences are value-laden systems,
plus the fact that the social scientist himself is
also a part of the subject matter being investigated.

In general, the issue is not that value assertions
are entirely irrelevant in any scientific discipline;
rather it is the manner in which a formal theory
structure is constructed and the *timing* when value
judgments or interpretations enter into the picture.
It is probably safe to say that in the end, a
matured discipline will have the capacity to encompass
both phases of operations—positive and normative,
but the former is necessarily the basis of the latter.
By a matured discipline, we mean that it has a common
core which is free of opinions and judgments and is
shared by most, if not all, of its students. The
students of such a discipline may disagree, as is
often the case, mostly in policy making and in
interpreting and evaluating a given problem or
unsettled situation. This means that judgmental
assertions are detachable from the theoretical
structure proper. The elegance and strength of a
positivistic system lies in its logical coherence
as well as empirical content but, most of all, in
its neutrality or objectivity with respect to
unanalyzable and unverifiable value statements.

With respect to the accounting discipline, we
recognize that both phases of operations—positive
and normative—are important. We believe, however,
that at the present time, the accounting theorist

in his attempt to find a formal structure should,
in general, subscribe to the modern empiricist
position concerning value statements (a value
judgment, of course), that is, to minimize the value
content of accounting propositions. The position
could be modified to include those normative,
ethical statements which have empirical correspondence
and are operative under a set of measures by
surrogation.[73] When postulates and constructs are
given a value content, value conclusions are
unavoidable. The danger of including the normative
type of statements or taking the "ought" position in
the construction of an accounting theory is that
the accountant will act as his own "referee" and
decide, for instance, what type of accounting
information users *ought to*, or *ought not to*, have.
The result is likely to deprive the user of freedom
and privilege of choosing the kind of data he
would like to have, if he had the opportunity to
observe and measure the given class of events
himself. Although it is not at all clear which
type of value symbols—descriptive or normative,
as distinguished by Ayer—is present in accounting
statements, we will do better, for the time being,
to leave value issues out of the structure of
accounting theory. In other words, what we
urgently need is a positive framework to guide us
in depicting, effectively and meaningfully, the
economic reality of specific accounting entities.
Short of empirical substantiation, normative
accounting must await the arrival of a positive

framework.   Treating accounting as a measurement
(or quasi-measurement) discipline, for instance,
requires that the accountant play the finder or
the measurer role first.   In general we believe
that it is theoretically significant to differentiate
and separate the positive and normative phases of
operations in accounting.   Diagram 5-1 illustrates
the respective places and relationships of these
two phases in the general area of the accounting
discipline.

It is often said that the scientist considers
only facts and their relations and that he keeps
emotive connotations out of his scientific investigation.   Emile Grunberg, in expounding the scope of
economic science, warns: "...The scientist is
rather concerned with its power to explain and
predict correctly, for the power [of science] to
control events is a by-product of successful
explanation."[74]   We do not wish to debate here the
issue of whether or not accounting is a science,
but we certainly are interested in the *methods* for
conducting research in a systematic way.   As
Kemeny so aptly puts it, "...the desire to find a
firm foundation for ethics is so strong that it
will even blind able thinkers to errors in their
logic."[75]

Diagram 5-1

Positive Accounting and Normative Accounting

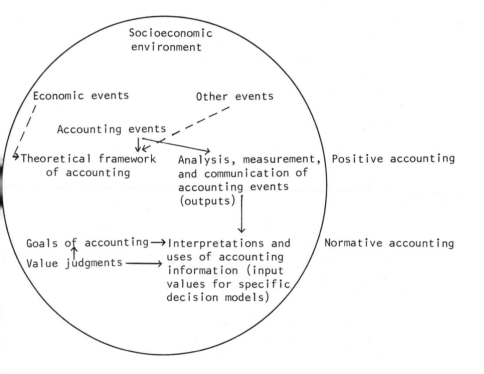

[1]A major part of this chapter with modifications and condensation was published in a paper entitled "The Several Modes of Normative Accounting Thought: A Critical Examination," *The International Journal of Accounting*, Spring, 1974, pp. 83-104.

[2]A general survey of these views is presented in the appendix at the end of the chapter.

[3]David Hume, *Treatise of Human Nature* (E. P. Dutton & Co., Inc., 1920, Everyman Edition), Vol. II, pp. 177-78.

[4]While differing from the position of this paper, Joseph Girard Louderback, III presents a comprehensive examination of the "fairness" concept and "experienced values" in his unpublished doctoral dissertation titled *Ethical Considerations in Accounting Theory Formulation*, University of Florida, 1970.

[5]DR Scott, "The Basis for Accounting Principles," *The Accounting Review*, December, 1941, pp. 341-349.

[6]Ibid.; see also his *The Cultural Significance of Accounts* (Columbia, Mo.: Lucas Brothers Publishers, n.d.), pp. 33 and 236-237.

[7]Paul Grady, *Inventory of Generally Accepted Accounting Principles for Business Enterprises*, Accounting Research Study No. 7 (New York: AICPA, 1965), pp. 54-55.

[8]James W. Pattillo, *The Foundation of Financial Accounting* (Baton Rouge: Louisiana State University Press, 1965), p. 27 and Chapter III.

[9]Ibid., p. 59.

[10]Ibid., pp. 58-59.

[11]"Comments of Leonard Spacek" in Robert T. Sprouse and Maurice Moonitz, *A Tentative Set of Broad Accounting Principles for Business Enterprises,* Accounting Research Study No. 3 (New York: AICPA, 1962), p. 78. See also "Comments of Leonard Spacek" in Maurice Moonitz, *The Basic Postulates of Accounting,* Accounting Research Study No. 1 (New York: AICPA, 1961), pp. 56-57; and Arthur Andersen & Co., *The Postulate of Accounting——What It Is, How It is Determined, How It Should Be Used* (Chicago: Arthur Andersen & Co., 1960).

[12] Grady, op cit., pp. 54-55.

[13] Accounting Principles Board, *Basic Concepts and Accounting Principles Underlying Financial Statements of Business Enterprises, Statement of the Accounting Principles Board, No. 4* (New York: AICPA, 1970), pp. 54 and 91.

[14]Committee on Auditing Procedure, *Auditing Standards and Procedures, Statement on Auditing Procedure No. 33* (New York: AICPA, 1963), pp. 69-74.

[15]William W. Werntz, "Accountant's Responsibility in Reporting Corporate Profits," *The Journal of Accountancy,* March, 1959, p. 47.

[16]This was well put by Charles E. Johnson and Robert N. Anthony in *Research in Accounting Measurement,* ed. Robert K. Jaedicke, Yuji Ijiri, and Oswald Nielsen (American Accounting Association, 1966), pp. 91 and 258.

[17]Committee on Accounting Procedure, "General Introduction and Rules Formerly Adopted," *Accounting Research Bulletin No. 1* (American Institute of Accountants, 1939), p. 1.

[18]William A. Paton and A. C. Littleton, *An Introduction to Corporate Accounting Standards* (American Accounting Association, 1940), pp. 2-3.

[19]A. C. Littleton and V. K. Zimmerman, *Accounting Theory: Continuity and Change* (Prentice-Hall, Inc., 1962), pp. 261-62.

[20]A Study Group at the University of Illinois, *A Statement of Basic Accounting Postulates and Principles* (Center for International Education and Research in Accounting, University of Illinois, 1964), pp. 2-3.

[21]E. Joe Demaris, "'Success-Indicator' Function of Income Concept Argues Its Further Development," *The Accounting Review*, January, 1963, p. 40.

[22]Norton M. Bedford, *Income Determination Theory: An Accounting Framework* (Addison-Wesley Publishing Company, Inc., 1965), Chapter 2 and pp. 20-23, 50-56.

[23]Ibid., p. 18.

[24]Committee to Prepare a Statement of Basic Accounting Theory, *A Statement of Basic Accounting Theory* (American Accounting Association, 1966), pp. 69-70.

[25]Yuji Ijiri, *The Foundations of Accounting Measurement* (Englewood Cliffs: Prentice-Hall, Inc., 1967), pp. 67 and 120.

[26]Carl Thomas Devine, "Research Methodology and Accounting Theory Formation," *The Accounting Review*, (July, 1960), pp. 397-99.

[27]Carl Thomas Devine, "Some Conceptual Problems in Accounting Measurements," *Research in Accounting Measurement*, op. cit., pp. 17-18.

[28]Alfred Rappaport, "Establishing Objectives for Published Corporate Accounting Reports," *The Accounting Review* (October, 1964), p. 954-61.

[29]David F. Linowes, "Socioeconomic Accounting," *The Journal of Accountancy* (November, 1968), pp. 37-48; and Sybil C. Mobley, "The Challenges of Socioeconomic Accounting," *The Accounting Review* (October, 1970), pp. 762-768.

[30]Mobley, ibid., p. 763.

[31]Committee to Prepare a Statement of Basic Accounting Theory, op. cit.

[32]Even systems analysts are beginning to experience difficulties from an increasing number of internal users and their diversified and insatiable needs.

[33]For a general review of the efficient market hypothesis, see Eugene F. Fama, "Efficient Capital Markets: A Review of Theory and Empirical Work," *Journal of Finance*, May 1970, pp. 383-417; Nicholas J. Gonedes, "Efficient Capital Markets and External Accounting," *The Accounting Review*, January, 1972, pp. 11-21; and William H. Beaver, "The Behavior of Security Prices and Its Implications for Accounting Research (Methods)," *Supplement to the Accounting Review*, 1972, pp. 407-437. There is a relatively large body of writings on this fashionable subject. The cited articles represent only a small sample.

[34]Fama, ibid., p. 385.

[35]Ray Ball, "Changes in Accounting Techniques and Stock Prices," *Emprical Research in Accounting: Selected Studies, 1972* (Supplement to Volume 10 of the *Journal of Accounting Research*), p. 2.

[36]Fama, op. cit., p. 383.

[37]For instance, see A. Rashad Abdel-Khalik, "The Efficient Market Hypothesis and Accounting Data: A Point of View," *The Accounting Review*, October, 1972, pp. 791-793; and David Downes and Thomas R. Dyckman, "A Critical Look at the Efficient Market Empirical Research Literature As It Relates to Accounting Information," *The Accounting Review*, April, 1973, pp. 300-317.

[38]Abdel-Khalik, ibid., p. 793.

[39]An expression used by Robert R. Sterling; see his "On Theory Construction and Verification," *The Accounting Review*, July, 1970, p. 453.

[40]Abdel-Khalik, op. cit., p. 793.

[41]Downes and Dyckman, op. cit., pp. 314-317.

[42]Stephen Zeff, "Comments on 'Varieties of Accounting Theory,'" *Foundations of Accounting Theory*, ed. Williard E. Stone. (University of Florida Press, 1971), p. 53.

[43]The following discussion is based on Louis Goldberg, "Varieties of Accounting Theory," Stone, ibid., pp. 31-49.

[44]Zeff, op. cit., p. 57.

[45]Kemeny, op. cit., p. 235.

[46]Lawrence Nabors, "The Positive and Genetic Approaches," *The Structure of Economic Science*, ed. Sherman Roy Krupp (Englewood Cliffs, N.J.: Prentice-Hall, Inc., 1966), p. 68.

[47]Raymond J. Chambers, *Accounting, Evaluation and Economic Behavior* (Englewood Cliffs, N.J.: Prentice-Hall, Inc., 1966), p. 1.

[48]Ibid., p. vi.

[49]Ibid., p. 40-42.

[50]Ibid., p. 41n.

[51]Ibid., pp. 20-21.

[52]Ibid., pp. 148-162.

[53]Moonitz, *The Basic Postulates of Accounting*, op. cit., pp. 2-6.

[54]For an extensive criticism on Moonitz's methodology, see Harvey T. Deinzer, *Development of Accounting Thought* (New York: Holt, Rinehart and Winston, Inc., 1965), pp. 108-111.

[55]Harold E. Arnett, "The Concept of Fairness," *The Accounting Review*, April, 1967, pp. 291-97.

[56]Curtis H. Stanley, *Objectivity in Accounting* (University of Michigan, 1965), pp. 12, 95, 102-105.

[57]F. R. Morgan, "Assumptions for Accountants," *Australian Accountant*, January, 1953, p. 32.

[58]F. Sewell Bray, "Accounting Dynamics," •*Accounting Research*, April, 1954, p. 138.

[59]William L. Raby, "The Two Faces of Accounting," *The Accounting Review*, July, 1959, p. 452-453.

[60]Ibid., pp. 455-456 and 460-461.

[61]George H. Sorter, "An Events Approach to Basic Accounting Theory," *The Accounting Review*, January, 1969, pp. 12-19.

[62]Ibid., p. 13.

[63]Ibid.

[64]Ibid., pp. 12 and 17.

[65]Orace Johnson "Toward an 'Events' Theory of Accounting," *The Accounting Review*, October, 1970, pp. 641-653.

[66]Goldberg, op. cit., pp. 35-36.

[67]Ibid., pp. 41-47.

[68]Ijiri, op. cit.

[69]Yuji Ijiri, "Logic and Sanctions in Accounting," *Accounting in Perspective*, ed. Robert R. Sterling and William F. Bentz (Cincinnatti: South-Western Publishing Co., 1971), pp. 3-28.

[70]Ibid., p. 5.

[71]Ibid., p. 26.

[72]Neal W. Klausner and Paul G. Kuntz, *Philosophy: The Study of Alternative Beliefs* (The Macmillan Company, 1961), p. 604.

[73]As such, these normative ethical statements would become "propositions" as defined previously.

[74]Emile Grunberg, "The Meaning of Scope and External Boundaries of Economics," ed. Krupp, op. cit., p. 149.

[75]Kemeny, op. cit., p. 235.

Appendix

Epistemological Foundations of
Normative Assertions
The Several Modes of Ethical Philosophy

With respect to the stream of ethical thought,
the several selected views are presented under three
main headings: (1) ethical thought of Greek
philosophers, (2) ethical thought of modern philosophy,
and (3) ethical positions of modern empiricism.

Ethical Thought of Greek Philosophers
The ethical thought of Greek philosophers has
a rather wide range. A group of thinkers in the fifth
and sixth centuries before Christ, known as the pre-
Socratics, were among the first to inquire about the
conditions of knowledge.[1] With largely metaphysical
views, they nevertheless planted the seeds of
rationalism and empiricism of western philosophy.
In addition, some of these early thinkers (for
instance, Pythagoras, Parmenides, and Heraclitus)
rendered significant influence upon the thought of

Plato and Aristotle. In the middle of the fifth
century B.C., a group of wandering teachers—the
Sophists—preached the art of persuasive speech.
The Sophists were skeptical of everything, including
objective standards and moral absolutes and became
the targets of the classic Greek philosophers'
criticism.

The classic Greek thought emphasized *reason*
as the basic criterion for knowledge. Perhaps no
philosopher in the classic group was more influential
upon most of the subsequent systems of the Greek
philosophy than Socrates. A sharp critic of the
Sophists, Socrates holds that there are objective
standards, established by means of logical reasoning,
for measuring our knowledge and conduct. He
distinguishes between the *particulars* of a kind and
the *essence* of the whole class. A standard is found
when the mind grasps this common essence or quality.
Socrates equates virtue with knowledge. Man will
do good if he knows what it is through reason;
vice or evil is the result of ignorance. As a
pupil of Socrates, Plato carried on his mentor's
distinction between the essence and the particulars
of a kind. Plato calls the universal or essence
"forms" or "ideas" which are the unchanging and
absolute values or realities. He equates absolute
values with the "good" against which actions are
judged. In his dialogues (first half of the fourth
century B.C.), Plato identifies virtue as the
fitness of a man for proper function in the world.
The human soul is governed by three virtues—

intellect, will, and emotion. But the ultimate
virtue is "justice" which provides the harmonic
relation of all the other virtues. The "just man,"
whose life is in the order of intellect, will, and
emotion, is the good man.

While Plato holds that the "real" is an eternal
and unchanging form, Aristotle emphasizes the concrete
world of facts and the concept of development. To
know what a thing is, we must know what it is
becoming. The final cause of Aristotle's concept
of development rests upon the Unmoved Mover who
engages in the most perfect activity—thinking,
that is,thinking about the highest. In his
Nichomachean Ethics (late fourth century B.C.), Aristotle
maintains that the unique attribute of man is reason
and that happiness results from the operation of
this attribute. Virtues essentially are habits.
Man must develop two kinds of habits in order to
attain happiness—habits of mental activity and
habits of practical action and emotion. The habits
of action can be developed in accordance with the
principle of moderation known as the "Golden Mean."
The Mean is defined as being between two extremes—
defect and excess.

Of the other Greek systems of moral philosophy,
two will be mentioned: Stoicism and Epicureanism.
The Stoics of Greece regarded man as a part of
nature which is orderly and is permeated with
reason. The good life of a man can be attained if
it is in harmony with nature. In the fourth and
third centuries B.C., Epicurus, an egoistic hedonist,

developed a system of thought known as Epicureanism,
which identified the highest good with pleasure,
particularly intellectual pleasure.   Epicurus
advocated an ascetic life devoted to contemplative
pursuits.   It may be noted that Epicurus contended
that knowledge is primarily the result of sense
perceptions—an anticipation of some of the features
of a later mode of thought: empiricism.

Ethical Thought of Modern Philosophy

Recognizing that the philosophical view of the
Middle Ages was, in general, theocentric and the
philosophy of the Renaissance was primarily
rationalistic with, among other things, a profound
interest in the viewpoint and values of ancient
Greece and Rome, let us move on to some of the
major systems of thought during the last three or
four centuries—an era in which modern philosophy
was born and has flourished.   It is a significant
period of philosophical development which has
produced some of the most able thinkers in human
history.   With respect to ethical thought, four
views will be presented: Spinozistic determinism,
formalism, utilitarianism, and evolutionism.

Spinozistic Determinism—It is beyond the scope
of this paper even to outline the arguments on
the nature of the universe and man's behavior
between the determinists and indeterminists.   At
the expense of oversimplification, we may say that
the extreme determinist would take the position
that everything in nature is determined by the
infinite mind.   Every fact or event in the universe

is guided by law and every effect must have a cause
(signifying the existence of causal laws). As such,
there is no free will, no free choice, and hence no
moral freedom. All human decision and choice, moral
or otherwise, is illusory. On the other hand, the
extreme indeterminists would take the opposite
position. Then there are moderate determinists
who would reject the rigid determinism in order to
save free will, including moral freedom, within
limits.

Our choice of a deterministic view here is
that of Benedict de Spinoza. With the rigor and
precision of mathematics (in the style of Euclidean
geometry—axioms, definitions, propositions, and
corollaries), Spinoza in his major work *Ethics*
(Ethica Ordine Geometrico Demonstrat, 1674) gives
the fullest expression of his metaphysical rationalistic
system of thought—the oneness of the infinite
substance of all things in terms of logical unity.[2]
The Spinozistic conception of substance is not
that of a material reality but of a metaphysical
entity; of the infinite attributes, he contends, only
two are apprehensible by the human mind—extension
and thought. All *particular* objects and ideas are
the modes of substance in these two attributes.
These modes are transient and finite, and their
existence assumes temporal form. When so viewed,
all particular things are found to be rigidly
necessary, precisely determined, and to exist in a
world of irrevocable causal processes. There is no
freedom or liberty. There is another aspect of all

things, however, that is, the *universal* aspect which
is eternal and infinite, and which transcends all
modal changes. This eternal world is not to be
found in the realm of existences (i.e., existent
things) but in that of essence which is nontemporal,
self-caused, universal, and immanent. It is only
in the latter that complete freedom is possible.

From this metaphysical context, Spinoza deduced
his ethical thought. It carries an eternal viewpoint
in that all things, including man, are morally
neutral. Only human needs and interests in the realm
of existences determine what men call good or evil,
right or wrong. Thus, when viewed from the particular
aspect, man is transitory and finite. When viewed
from the universal aspect, man is a necessary
part of the Infinite or God, and, as such, he is no
longer enslaved by circumstances, that is, he frees
himself from his delimiting particularity. For
Spinoza, there is still a higher form of knowing,
namely, intuition. The highest human state is the
"intellectual love of God" through intuitive understanding. By the proper use of this faculty, man
may contemplate the infinite substance. In general,
man should view his life *sub specie aeternitatis*
(under the aspect of eternity). Thus, to fulfill
his destiny, man must forego passing or temporary
good and search for the enduring good.

Formalism — Probably few philosophers during the
past two centuries have made a deeper impression
upon their followers than has Emmanuel Kant. Kant's

ethical theory, known as formalism, affirms that
moral action is guided by man's reason (Kant used
the term "rational beings" rather than men, signifying
his intention to stress the universality of a rational
law).[3] According to Kant, man intuitively knows right
from wrong in moral actions, and it is the moral
motive of *duty* that determines whether an act is
good or not. The rightness of any action is universal,
binding on all rational minds. Thus, like rational
knowledge, rational morality is a priori. To Kant,
the necessary or categorical nature of the moral
good obligates the knower to proceed not from
inclination, but from a sense of duty which is based
on a general principle that is right in itself. Kant
rejects relativism in ethics based on observation,
experience, or consequences and maintains that the
test of a moral act in the light of a moral principle
is a logical one. Kant's duty-bound thought of ethics
also reveals his position in holding that *ought*
statements are independent and autonomous, as contrasted
to the position held by some moral philosophers that
ought statements are based upon *is* statements.
Thus, to Kant, a moral law is autonomous and pre-
scriptive.

Utilitarianism—The mode of thought concerning moral
quality in terms of pleasure and pain is generally
known as hedonism (from the Greek word for pleasure,
hedone, which means "sweet"). Of the several systems
of hedonism, perhaps the most noted and influential
is utilitarianism (or universalism), which stresses

the social nature of ethical behavior and holds that
the ethical concept is a product of society. Man
thinks not only of his own good but also of the
social good of others. The two foremost utilitarians
are Jeremy Bentham and John Stuart Mill. While
differing in forms of exposition, both criticized
the use of reason as a criterion for developing
ethical theories and maintained that questions of
ultimate ends are not amenable to direct proof.

By appealing to the naturalism of Epicurus,
Bentham holds that pleasure and pain are experienced.
Unlike Epicurus' egoistic hedonism, however,
Bentham's hedonistic thought connotes a universal
tone. Written at the time of the French Revolution,
Bentham's *Introduction to the Principles of Morals
and Legislation* sets forth the "principle of utility"
as an ideological tool in terms of augmenting the
happiness of the community.[4] To Bentham, democracy
rests upon equal value of pleasure and pain, and
upon the number of persons to whom pleasure and
pain are extended. It may be noted that the
utilitarian mode of thought was expounded earlier
by David Hume and John Locke. It is to Bentham's
credit, however, that he attempted to make the
slogan of the highest good of utilitarianism "the
greatest pleasure of the greatest number of people"
precise.

Mill continued "the multiplication of happiness,"
and emphasized experiential or psychological pleasure
and "desirability." To Mill, the morality of an
individual action is a question of the application
of a fundamental principle at the root of all

morality.[5] Is this an a priori or a posteriori
principle? Mill elects to follow the inductive
method. He argues that the ethical concept,
"justice," can be analyzed through acts in an
empirical manner and that justice is partially
dependent upon utility. It is interesting to note
that the utilitarian does not offer to define
"pleasure." What he says is, in essence, that "good
is pleasure" and "pleasure is good."[6] As criticized
by G. E. Moore, what the hedonist is actually
saying is that "pleasure is pleasure," unless the
expression "pleasure is good" means that good is
something other than pleasure.[7]

Evolutionism—The scientific development since the
seventeenth century has rendered significant impact
on ethical theories. For instance, Sir Isaac Newton's
discoveries were thought of as clues that there is a
rational and orderly divine nature upon which a system
of ethics rests. Probably the scientific development
that most affected ethics is Charles Darwin's theory
of evolution—"survival of the fittest." The British
philosopher, Herbert Spencer, used Darwin's findings
to establish the ethical system commonly known as
"evolutionary ethics." Spencer contends that
morality is the product of evolution. By elaborating
Darwin's thesis, Friedrich W. Nietzche advocates that
the so-called moral conduct is necessary only to a
weak society. In the twentieth century, Julian
Huxley is regarded as the one most noted for
advancing the evolutionary theory of ethics.[8] Huxley

claims that actions based on ethical maxims will
expedite evolution, and that everyone ought to have
an equal opportunity to develop himself. In
anthropological studies, evolutionary principles
of ethics have been applied to affirm the relativistic
concept of ethics, effecting the belief that
different societies possess different systems of
mores.

While there are other modes of evolutionistic
thought of ethics, the above presentation shows that
it is difficult to reconcile the various evolutionary
systems of ethics. In an oversimplified manner, we
may say that under the evolutionary view, good is
synonymous with nature. Since reality is not
knowable, we can only know the appearances in nature.
As a part of nature, man must accept only those
moral obligations consistent with his nature. In
trusting nature, we find that happiness and progress
result from the evolution of nature.

Ethical Positions of Modern Empiricism

Of the various systems of modern empiricism,
three will be noted: William James' pragmatism,
John Dewey's instrumentalism, and logical positivism.

Pragmatism and Instrumentalism—Before proceeding
to the view of logical positivism on ethical
assertions, it may be worthwhile to note briefly
two other variants of modern empiricism—William
James' pragmatism and John Dewey's instrumentalism.[9]
As a psychologist and philosopher, James holds that
man's behavior is motivated by pleasure or happiness

and that good is evaluated in terms of the consequences
of an action in advancing human well-being. For
ethical theory, he places the same degree of emphasis
on the importance of interrelationships in ideas as
in other phenomena. Dewey's "reciprocity of means
and ends" mode of thought maintains that any concept
of ultimate good is meaningless. Instead, good is
evaluated in terms of the result reflecting upon
both the means and the probable consequences of
realizing the good. Further, the good must meet
the test of social verification—the same methods
of verification through which all other facts are
established. Since society changes, the idea of
good changes too.

Logical Positivism——The several modes of ethical
thought presented so far have at least one thing
in common, that is, to find a firm foundation
(metaphysical, rationalistic, or experiential) for
ethical assertions. A powerful group of modern
philosophers, known as logical positivists, challenges
the validity of ethical statements. In general,
they hold that the truth-value of an ethical statement
cannot be established either through analysis of the
meaning of the words used or through empirical verification. As such, it is neither a logical construct
nor an empirical generalization. Consequently, there
is no criterion which can be used to determine its
validity. Thus, to the logical empiricist, value
statements are unanalyzable, unverifiable, and meaningless. Alfred Jules Ayer claims that ethical concepts

are mere "pseudo concepts."[10] He distinguishes two
types of value statements, however: (1) those with
purely *normative* ethical symbols and (2) those with
descriptive ethical symbols.[11] The former express
ethical judgments of an individual and have no
factual content whatsoever; the latter simply state
types of conduct in the light of a given (or presupposed
society's value system, and hence are not merely
judgmental assertions.   Charles Stevenson differentiates
agreement (or disagreement) between beliefs and
between attitudes.   He says that agreement or
disagreement between beliefs "is concerned with how
matters are truthfully to be described and explained,"
while the argument between attitudes "is concerned
with how they are to be favored or disfavored,..."[12]

A common criticism of logical positivism is the
doubtfulness of a sharp distinction between "cognitive
meaning" and "emotive meaning." Modern philosophers
are by no means in agreement as to whether such a
division is possible, and some (e.g., William James
and Alfred North Whitehead) assert a continuity and
overlap of cognition and emotion. In addition,
critics of logical positivism find that whatever
the positivist does not care to consider, he regards
as meaningless.[13]

[1]Milton Charles Nahm, ed., *Selections from Early Greek Philosophers* (Appleton-Century-Crofts, 1934).

[2]Benedict de Spinoza, *Ethics: Proved in Geometrical Order* (New York: E. P. Dutton & Co. Inc.), 1938.

[3]*Kant's Critique of Practical Reason*, trans. T. K. Abbott, (New York: Green & Co., Inc., 1927), pp. 2-48.

[4]Jeremy Bentham, *The Principles of Morals and Legislation* (New York: Hafner Publishing Co., Inc., 1948).

[5]John Stuart Mill, *Utilitarianism* (New York: The Liberal Arts Press, Inc., 1949), pp. 2-34.

[6]Ibid., pp. 2-4.

[7]W. Sellars and John Hospers, eds., *Readings in Ethical Theory* (New York: Appleton-Century-Crofts, 1952), p. 70.

[8]Julian S. Huxley, *Evolutionary Ethics* (New York: Oxford University Press, 1943).

[9]William James, "The Moral Philosopher and the Moral Life," *Pragmatism and Other Essays* (New York: Washington Square Press, Inc., 1963); John Dewey, *The Quest for Certainty* (London: George Allen & Unwin, Ltd., 1930); _____, *Logic, The Theory of Inquiry* (New York: Holt, Rinehart & Winston, Inc., 1938); and _____, "Theory of Valuation," *International Encyclopedia of Unified Science*, Vol. II, No. 4 (Chicago: University of Chicago Press, 1939).

[10]Alfred Jules Ayer, *Language, Truth and Logic* (New York: Dover Publications, Inc., 1952), p. 107.

[11]Ibid., pp. 105-106.

[12]Charles Stevenson, *Ethics and Language* (New Haven, Conn.: Yale University Press, 1944), p. 4.

[13]Philip Blair Rice, *On the Knowledge of Good and Evil* (New York: Random House, 1955), p. 61.

6 Measurement and Accounting

It has often been said that all scientists
engage in quantitative operations of one kind or
another. During the past several decades we have
witnessed conscientious efforts made by philosophers
of science, mathematicians, and physical and social
scientists to develop and expand the meaning, theory,
rules, and instruments of measurement; however,
the seeming clarity, simplicity, orderliness, and
operativeness of the concept of measurement is a very
complicated matter. Students of measurement have
not, through the years, reached a common definition
of measurement. For instance, the clash of opinions
on the issue of measurability of "quantitative
estimates of sensory events" caused the British
Assocaition for the Advancement of Science to
appoint a special committee to deliberate on this

matter in 1932. This distinguished committee
spent most of its time on the *meaning* of measurement,
and its Final Report published in 1940 showed a wide
split on this matter.[1] The debate on the meaning
of measurement, as well as on its scales and
dimensions, among scientists continues to this
day.

Whether accounting is a science or not,
measurement is not only relevant but crucial to
accounting operations. The reason is twofold.
First, accounting quantifies certain economic events.
Secondly, the basic function of accounting is to
provide information, and quantitative measurement
(in contrast to qualitative measurement) makes
"information more informative."[2] Although accounting
is not yet a measurement discipline in a scientific
sense, contemporary accounting literature attests
impressively that accountants are busy with learning
and applying this body of knowledge to accounting.
The purpose of this chapter is to examine the
concept, theory, and process of measurement, with
particular reference to their applicability to
accounting. Because there is a vast body of
knowledge in measurement including different
viewpoints, our discussion in this syllabus is
necessarily general and hence serves only as an
introduction to measurement theory and process.

Meaning and Characteristics of Measurement

To measure is, with the use of proper
apparatus, to ascertain the dimensions, relations,
and capacities of objects or properties in symbolic

or quantitative terms. The process of measurement itself consists of a system, the measurer, and the object being measured. This is an oversimplified explanation of measurement, however, especially in an operational sense. Scientists are widely divided on what constitutes measurement. This situation reflects, in part at least, why we measure, how we measure, and what can be measured. The lack of a general definition of measurement is due largely to the conceptual diversity of viewpoints on objects and properties to be measured, particularly between those in the physical sciences and those in the social sciences. The clash between Norman R. Campbell (a physicist) and S. S. Stevens (a psychologist) in respect to this definitional matter exemplifies how difficult it is to find a common meaning of measurement.

It is not possible to trace its origin, but there is no doubt that measurement, as it stands today, evolved from the number system. The so-called classical measurement theory was developed in the physical sciences from which it was extended, modified, and applied to the social sciences. The classical view, of which Campbell is a leading figure, presents, relatively speaking, a narrow concept of measurement. In essence, it places the emphasis on the differences between direct or "fundamental" measurement and "derived" or "dependent" measurement; the latter is a process of measurement which calls for references to "fundamental magnitudes." It refuses to recognize anything as measurement other than the procedures involved in the two types of measurement described.

In addition, this view holds that objects possess
a priori properties "in virtue of the laws governing
these properties."[3] The classical view confines
measurement to objects of the physical world, but
measurement in the area of the social sciences
requires a broader view. In this respect, Stevens'
definition of measurement has often been cited.
According to Stevens, measurement is defined as
"the assignment of numerals to objects or events
according to rule—any rule."[4] The emphasis is
placed on the mathematical properties of numerical
assignment and the scaling or leveling of measurement. Stevens' definition has been criticized as
too broad on the ground that numerals can be
assigned to any object whether measurable or not.
Furthermore, his use of the last two words of his
definition, "any rule," is too loose, gives no
direction, and hence is meaningless. Moreover,
to many measurement theorists, Stevens' "nominal"
scale (classification) of measurement is not
measurement at all.

      In addition to the two views presented above,
there are other variations in respect to the
concept and process of measurement. Indeed, the
subject of measurement has been expounded so
widely in scientific literature that a reconciliation
of the various viewpoints is not possible at present.
It should be noted that these various versions of
measurement do not necessarily exclude one another
to the extreme, but they overlap to a great extent.
Thus, there are certain common characteristics of

measurement from which we may gain some insights
into the nature, meaning, and function of measurement.
Following is a general recapitulation of some of
these characteristics. First, measurement requires
an identification of objects and their properties to
be measured. This is the initial step of all
measurement processes. Second, not all objects and
properties are measurable. This calls for a clear
distinction between constitutive definitions and
operational definitions of objects or properties—
a basic theme of the so-called operationalism.
Third, measurement is the assignment of symbols,
usually numerals to objects according to rules.
Thus, in addition to identifying the property to
be measured, measurement rules specify the scale
to be used, and the dimension of the measuring
unit. This is the quantitative aspect of measurement. Fourth, the assignment of symbols or numerals
to objects is a process of substitution. The
relations among the numerals assigned hold if,
only if, the relations of the objects or properties
are established first. This means that the relations
among the numerals must be specified and assigned
in order to represent the relations of the objects
or properties. Thus we must obtain an isomorphism
(i.e., one-to-one correspondence) in the measurement process "between certain characteristics of
the number system involved and the relations
between various quantities (instances) of the
property to be measured."[5] Fifth, the essence of
measurement is to reveal, symbolically or

quantitatively, relations among objects. The
assignment of a number to a single object does
not give us any information or meaning, unless it
can be compared with numbers assigned to other
objects possessing certain relations among these
objects.[6] Lastly, but definitely not the least,
measurement is founded on the theoretical framework of specific disciplines. As Robert R. Sterling
puts it, "Theory without measurement is mere
speculation... Measurement without theory is
aimless wandering."[7]

Scales of Measurement

Scales of measurement specify levels at
which measurement is made. One of the scaling
issues is what constitutes the lowest level or
minimum of measurement. Levels of measurement
progress as we move from one scale to the next.
There are various systems of measurement scales,
of which the scale systems of Warren S. Torgerson,
Clyde H. Coombs, and S. S. Stevens are the three
most widely followed ones. Of the three systems,
reference to Stevens' is probably made most
frequently. For our purposes here, we shall follow
Stevens' system with a brief comparison with some
of the other systems.

Stevens presents four scales of measurement:
(1) nominal, (2) ordinal, (3) interval, and (4)
ratio, as shown in Table 6-1. Let us examine each
in turn.[8]

Nominal scale. Stevens includes the assignment
of numerals at the classification level as a scale

Table 6-1*

Scales of Measurement

The basic operations needed to create a given scale are all those listed
in the second column, down to and including the operation listed opposite
the scale. The third column gives the mathematical transformations that
leave the scale form invariant. Any numeral x on a scale can be replaced
by another numeral x', where x' is the function of x listed in column 3.
The fourth column lists, cumulatively downward, some of the statistics
that show invariance under the transformations of column 3.

Scale	Basic Empirical Operations	Mathematical Group Structure	Permissible Statistics (invariantive)	Typical Examples
Nominal	Determination of equality	Permutation group $x' = f(x)$ [$f(x)$ means any one-to-one substitution]	Number of cases Mode Contingency correlation	"Numbering" of football players Assignment of type or model numbers to classes
Ordinal	Determination of greater or less	Isotonic group $x' = f(x)$ [$f(x)$ means any increasing monotonic function]	Median Percentiles Order correlation (type O)	Hardness of minerals Quality of leather, lumber, wool, etc. Pleasantness of odors
Interval	Determination of equality of intervals or differences	General linear group $x' = ax + b$	Mean Standard deviation Order correlation (type I) Product-moment correlation	Temperature (Fahrenheit and centigrade) Energy Calendar dates "Standard scores" on achievement tests (?)
Ratio	Determination of equality of ratios	Similarity group $x' = ax$	Geometric mean Coefficient of variation Decibel transformations	Length, weight, density, resistance, etc. Pitch scale (mels) Loudness scale (sones)

*S. S. Stevens, "Mathematics, Measurement, and Psychophysics," *Handbook
of Experimental Psychology*, ed. S. S. Stevens (John Wiley & Sons, Inc.,
1951), p. 25.

of measurement. This scale is for identifying
individuals (as in the case of numbering football
players) and for "numbering" types or classes of
objects, where each member of a class is assigned
the same number. The numbering of classes of
objects or events is based on the demonstration of
equality in respect to trait or the like. In
other words, classification of diverse objects can
be made only if they have some property in common
(e.g., male and female classification). When
there exist numerous properties, each common
property may serve as a basis for further classifying
or categorizing (e.g., different roles played by a
person). Classification must be made for certain
meaningful purposes (e.g., for paving the way to
compare or bring out relations among the classes
at advanced scales). Under a nominal scale, the
relation of equality must be symmetric and transitive.
Symmetry means that, if the relation holds between
a and *b*, *a* = *b*, it also holds between *b* and *a*.
Transitivity means that if *a* = *b* and *b* = *c*, then
a = *c*. This symmetric transformation reveals that
the structure of the scale remains invariant when
any two designating numerals are interchanged.
Stevens calls it a "permutation group" because
there is no rank order involved in a nominal scale
(e.g., as *abc* into *acb*, *bac*, etc.).

Classification of objects or events is no
trivial matter. To Stevens, "an operation for
determining equality is obviously the first step
in measurement.... Without this step, no further
measurement would be possible."[9] It forms the basis

for categorizing and conceptualizing objects, for
coding and recording information, and for identifying,
sorting, and labeling events. Nominal scaling is
very much related to information theory which, among
other things, provides a tool for the treatment of
data of alternative categories at the nominal level
of measurement. To Stevens, classification is a
form of measurement in the sense that the assignment
of numerals to classes is not made in a "random"
manner, but is made according to rule. The rule
is: "Do not assign the same numerals to different
classes or different numerals to the same class."[10]

The inclusion of the nominal scale as a level
of measurement is a much debated issue among the
students of measurement. Many of them contend that
it is too primitive to be recognized as measurement
and that the example given by Stevens, numbering
football players, does not yield a measurement. In
other words, the nominal scale is not scaling at
all, but is merely a way of renaming objects by
numerals. All objects or events can be numbered,
whether or not they are measurable. As such,
nominal scaling is not quantifying, and classification can be made effectively by qualitative terms
or definitions. Recognizing that the nominal scale
is a primitive form of measurement, Stevens notes
its usefulness in various scientific researches
and contends that it is within the definition of
measurement.

Ordinal Scale. The ordinal scale is the level
of measurement at which we rank or order objects

according to the relative (greater or lesser amount
of a particular property that they possess. Order
relation is made in terms of equivalence, comparability, and consistency. The numbering of a series
could be designated by 1, 2, 3, 4, 5, ... or by
letters, a, b, c, d, e, ... Ordering in numerical
terms is always preferred, because qualitative
ordering is not only vague and somewhat arbitrary,
but most of all, it contains a psychological and
judgmental factor. For instance, we may rank
"temperature" as coldest, colder, cold, cool,
lukewarm, warm, hot, hotter, and hottest. What is
cool to one person, however, may be cold to
another. Thus, it is more objective and informative
to assign numerical scales to temperature readings.
Instead of saying cool and cold, we say that 60°
is a greater or higher reading than 50° or that
50° is less or lower than 60°. The same goes for
"hardness," "grades of same object," "weight,"
and "length."

Although we can almost always classify any
object, not all properties can be ranked in order
or used for classification purposes simultaneously.
Certainly, weight and length can be measured in
both qualitative and numerical terms, but not
properties like shape and color. We can say A is
heavier than, or longer than, B. We can say that
two shapes are equivalent or identical, but not
that one is "shaper" than the other, such as
saying that one "square" is squarer than, or less
square than, another square. Similarly, a red
object cannot be ranked as redder than, or less

red than, a green object.   This explains that
ranking is done in terms of a specific or common
property only.   Shape and color are independent
properties which are unrankable.

The ordinal scale has the mathematical property
of invariance, since any order-preserving transformation will leave invariant the relation of
"betweenness" for a given value with respect to its
neighbors on the scale, signifying the structure
of an isotonic group.   Data so measured under the
ordinal scale provide the kind of information which
enables us to choose among alternatives.

Interval Scale.   The ordinal scale enables us
to order or compare a class of objects, but it
does not tell us the exact magnitude of a property.
As such, the ordinal scale does not provide answers
to the following questions: How cold is cold?
How heavy is heavy?   How high is high?   Is it too
cold or not too cold?   The "temperature" example
we used previously gives no indication as to the
interval difference, or linear distance between
50° and 60° without knowing the full range of
temperature.   These magnitudes are indeterminate
under the ordinal scale.   To have more information
we must progress to the next scale—the interval.
The interval scale provides a range with upper and
lower limits of the magnitude of a property, so
that the differences marked with equidistance
(equal intervals) between different amounts (or
distances) of a property are positioned and measured.
We can determine equal differences as *10 - 5 =*

8 - 3. The interval scale consists of the real
numbers and a linear function *(x' = ax + b, a > 0,*
where *x* denotes any numeral on the scale and can
be replaced by another numeral *x'*, and *x'* is the
function of *x* as indicated in the linear equation).
The Fahrenheit scale of measuring temperature and
the scales of calendar time are good examples of
the interval scale of measurement. A numerical
value on the Fahrenheit scale or a date on one
calendar may be transformed, respectively, to that
on another by means of the linear equation. The
fact that there are four interval scales with
different zero positions to measure changes in
temperature (i.e., Fahrenheit, Centigrade, Rakine
and Kelvin) is merely a matter of choosing the
unit of measure and the place (except the Kelvin
scale, which has a natural zero point set at -273°C).
This brings out an important point about the interval
scale. The zero position on an interval scale is
arbitrarily assigned. It does not represent a
true "zero" of a given property. As such, any
given number (a constant) can be added without
destroying the relations between intervals, that is,
the scale form remains invariant. Thus, the interval
scale has the structure of a linear or an affined
group (a transformation that yields "paralleling
effects.")

    Ratio Scale. The ratio scale is used to
measure the *relative* relations between objects.
It remains *constant* without regard to their
absolute values. Numerals are assigned in such a
way that equal ratios (e.g. *10/5 = 8/4*, etc.) among

themselves correspond to equal ratios of some
attribute or other. For instance, the ratio of a
dollar to a dime is *1:10*. Unlike the interval
scale, the zero on a ratio scale represents the
base, and as such the zero place is the absolute
zero position of the scale. The interval scale
becomes a ratio scale when the zero is assigned
an absolute value. The only thing that is arbitrary
on a ratio scale is the unit of measurement. In
other words, a ratio scale is an interval scale
with an added property: its origin is an absolute
zero. With a proper measuring unit (e.g., pound,
ton, foot, or meter), ratios of the numbers are
obtained by reference to the zero base on the scale.
Thus the ratio scale is, in essence, an advancement
of the interval scale in terms of equal ratios.
The mathematical group structure of the numerical
values of a ratio scale is represented by $x' = ax$,
where $c > 0$. That is to say, its numerical values
can be transformed (e.g., from ounces to pounds or
from inches to feet) by multiplying each value by
a constant without alternating their respective
proportions.

The ratio scale is the highest of Stevens'
scales of measurement. Given the property for
measuring objects and the unit of measure, the
ratio scale is unique in the sense that it classifies
every object by the number assigned to it on the
scale, such that ratio comparisons can be made. It
should be noted that Stevens' four scales are cumulative in the sense that to an empirical operation
with the use of a given scale must be added all

those operations of the preceding scales. For
instance, the establishment of an interval scale
(equating or differentiating intervals) is preceded
by a procedure for determining the equality of a
given class of objects (i.e., the nominal scale),
plus a procedure for ascertaining the relative
amount of a given property (i.e., the ordinal
scale). Thus the power of each scale advances as it
moves to the next one. In addition to the four
scales, Stevens also mentioned the "logarithmic
interval scale" (which he calls the "power group"
represented by the expression $x' = kx^n$, where k
and n are constants and must be positive) but found
it to be useless to the empirical business of
science.[11]

A word is in order about two other widely
followed systems of measurement scales without
elaboration—the systems of Clyde H. Coombs and
Warren S. Torgerson, respectively.[12] Coombs also
includes "classification" as a scale of measurement.
In addition to Stevens' four scales, however, Coombs
added seven more scales, including the "partially
ordered scale" which falls between the nominal scale
and the ordinal scale. Thus, Coombs' measurement
system contains eleven scales. Torgerson does
not include "classification" as a scale of
measurement and considers the ordinal scale as the
lowest level of measurement. His last two scales
being identical with Stevens' (the interval and
ratio scales), Torgerson subdivided Stevens'
ordinal scale into one without a natural origin

and one with a natural origin, this latter scale
is assumed to have the number zero representing
a zero quantity of a property.

Kinds of Measurement

As originally conceived by Campbell,[13]
physical scientists have conventionally classified
measurement into two types: fundamental and
derived. By fundamental measurement, we mean that
properties can be measured independently; and, in
addition, they possess the characteristic of
additivity. By derived measurement, we mean those
properties whose magnitudes are measured in terms
of certain *fundamental* magnitudes. Magnitudes
represented by fundamental scales in physics are
few in number, such as weight, length, electrical
resistance, and the like. To this we may also
add numerosity. Derived magnitudes are more
numerous in physics than fundamental magnitudes.
Typical derived scales are represented by density,
velocity, and elasticity. Both "fundamental" and
"derived" scales use ratio scales.

As an illustration, suppose we wish to measure
the densities of gasoline, alcohol, water, hydrochloric
acid, and mercury.[14] By experiment, we know that
their densities vary from one another and that
these liquids can be arranged in a series of
increasing density. We could assign five numbers
(1, 2, 3, 4, 5) to designate the density scale of
these liquids. These numbers are arbitrarily
chosen, however, and we cannot say that liquid *A*
assigned number *1* is twice as dense as liquid *B*

assigned number *2*, or vice versa. Density is not
an additive property of a liquid. So there must
be another way in which numbers are not arbitrarily
chosen——the existence of a numerical law. Experi-
mentally we have found that the *ratio* of the numbers
measuring different weights and volumes of a liquid
is the *same*, no matter how large or small the volume
we measure. The law is $W = cV$, with W being the
measure of the weight, V, that of the corresponding
volume, and c, a constant for all samples of the same
liquid. By proper choice of the units of weight
and volume, we find that c has the value *.75* for
alcohol, *1.00* for water, *1.27* for hydrochloric
acid, and *13.6* for mercury. The order of the ratios
is the same as the aforementioned ordering, but
the measures are obtained without arbitrariness to
the differences in density. But density, no matter
how measured, is a nonadditive property (we should
not say that the density of mercury is *13.6* times
that of water).

The theory structure of the physical sciences
contains many formal laws, and the assignment of
numerals to fundamental and derived magnitudes is
made operationally in the light of these laws.
In contrast, the theoretical framework of the social
sciences is vague, inexact, and much less formal.
There are no such things as "laws" in the strictest
sense in the social sciences. Consequently, the
basic ingredients of measurement in the social
sciences (such as the truth value of social concepts,
operational definitions, identifiableness of measurable

properties, the extent to which measuring scales
can be established—for example, the determination
of an absolute zero value or, to a lesser extent,
of equal distances or differences, and the exact
relations of classes of objects or events) are
quite imprecise. Because of this, the social
scientist rarely measures in terms of either the
fundamental or the derived type of measurement.

However, the social scientist measures anyway,
but with a lesser degree of precision. But what
kind of measurement is it? Warren S. Torgerson
explains this in the following manner. Although
"fundamental measurement is a means by which numbers
can be assigned according to natural laws to
represent the property and yet which does not pre-
suppose measurement of any other variables," and
derived measurement is conducted "*through laws
relating the* property to other properties," the
characteristics of order, distance, and origin
may obtain meaning by a kind of measurement with
the use of arbitrary definition, and we might call
this "measurement by fiat."[15] The difficulty in
dealing with socioeconomic phenomena is the inexactness of relationships among variables, which may or
may not bear out the consequences of further observations and which may or may not be measurable in
terms of quantitative scales. The term "arbitrary
definition" connotes a prescientific notion,
lacking in preciseness in terms of its operational
properties and in terms of its relations with others.
Thus measurement by fiat enables us to engage in

the kind of measurement based on *our* definitions
of concepts, objects, or events (i.e., not in
terms of any natural laws) interacted with our
limited ability of observation, and vice versa.
When objects are defined in a variety of ways,
measurement on a definitional basis will yield
alternative possibilities and, hence, various sets
of relations among variables. The ideal situation
is, of course, that if the alternative operations
give us the same result, the arbitrariness of
definitions would be of little significance, but
ideal often remains ideal.

Measurement in Quantum Mechanics and Its Relevance
to Accounting Measurement

     The development of quantum theory and quantum
mechanics has caused some fundamental changes in
the concepts of Newtonian classical mechanics.[16]
It has produced lengthy debates on the theoretical
validity, as well as the philosophical foundation,
of classical physics as a universally adequate
system of explanation in a deterministic way. It
has cast doubt on the possibility of discovering
scientific laws of causal relations (i.e., the "if
a then *b* pattern" of causal orders—the scientist's
dream). The state of modern quantum theory, however,
is still uncertain. Some noted physicists (including
Planck, Einstein, and De Broglie) have serious
reservations about the theory. For instance, we do
not know whether it is in its final, definite stage
(i.e., "Nature may very well be as the quantum
physicist describes it."[17]) or whether it is still

in a transitional stage, that is, a part of
something larger. It has been regarded as a statistical theory, implying, among other things,
that many times in the history of science a new
theory started out as statistical and progressed
later to a precise theory. Taking the present
state of quantum theory, however, the social
scientist, who has through the years envied the
research methodology and exactness of the physical
sciences and has tried to apply many of their
concepts and techniques to the social sciences,
may take not only a great deal of comfort from the
probabilistic element of quantum theory but, most
of all, may be in a better position to apply some
of the ideas of quantum theory to his own area of
study, especially in measuring and explaining
phenomena of the human world. For this very
reason, we shall look into some of the relevant
features of quantum theory in the hope that an
awareness of it may sharpen and benefit our measurement of human events in general and accounting
events (which are a subclass of the former) in
particular. In the discussion that follows, we
shall concentrate mostly on some of the postulates
and hypotheses of quantum mechanics.

   Quantum mechanics was formulated simultaneously
by Schrodinger in the form of a simple differential
equation and by Heisenberg in the form of matrices.
It is highly abstract in mathematical terms and,
as such, its hypotheses are deductively derived,
attempting to interpret subatomic objects. In

light of its postulates, it is a statistical
theory, reflecting a transition from causal laws
to probability calculations. A most important
feature of the theory is the inseparability of the
observed and the observer, resulting in an
"interaction" of the object to be measured and
the measuring apparatus. This is in contrast to
the view of classical mechanics, which holds that
the observer stands quite outside of any physical
system and does not affect the system itself. With
or without measurement, the classical mechanical
system holds not only that values in definite
terms can be assigned to position, energy, velocity,
and so on, but that their values are independent
of one another. In addition, these values "can be
measured accurately, and the results can be
combined to give a complete, coherent, and detailed
description of the State."[18] Any errors from
measuring instruments can be, in principle, calculated
and corrected. This sharp separation of the observed
and the observer is assumed away in quantum mechanics.
Instead, the observed and the observer form together
a *larger* system signifying their "interaction" which
affects the value of the object measured. Properties
of subatomic elements (the subject matter of quantum
theory) in some situations possess the characteristics
of *particles*, and in other situations, the characteristics of *waves*. These properties give the
"dual nature" of the subatomic elements, which
according to the theory, cannot be measured
simultaneously with precise values. This hypothesis,
deduced from the assumptions of the theory, is

the well-known, celebrated Heisenberg's "uncertainty
principle" which has justifiably or unjustifiably
labeled the quantum theory "indeterministic."

One of these uncertainty relations is expressed
in the following formula: $\Delta p \cdot \Delta q \geq h/4\pi$ in which
p and q usually are read as the coordinates of
"position" and "momentum," respectively, of subatomic elements (e.g. electrons, protons, and so
on). The coefficients of dispersions of values
obtained by measurement are denoted by Δp and Δq,
respectively; and h is Planck's constant. At any
given instant, the product of the dispersions of
the position and momentum of a subatomic element is
never less than $h/4\pi$. The uncertainty principle
asserts that if one of the coordinates is measured
with a high degree of precision, it is not possible
to obtain simultaneously a precise value for the
conjugate coordinate. The two are not independent
of each other, that is, the equations of quantum
mechanics cannot establish a unique correspondence
between positions and momenta at different points
of time. When extended, the uncertainty principle
simply says that we must abandon the universal
schemes in explanation of classical mechanics that
all phenomena have spatiotemporal relations between
objects. "The observable prediction of the theory
can be described approximately in such terms, but
not uniquely.... This indeterminateness of the
picture of the process is a direct result of the
indeterminateness of the concept 'observation'—
it is not possible to decide, other than arbitrarily,
what objects are to be considered as part of the

observer's apparatus."[19]   Instead, quantum theory
calculates the *probability* of the specified
momentum of a particle when it has a certain
position. As such, the theory, as it goes, is
inherently statistical in nature. The uncertainty
principle contends that the interaction between the
object and the measurement instruments causes
"uncontrollable and larger changes in the systems
being measured," that the act of measurement
itself destroys the original system, and that what
we have measured is the resulting "interaction."[20]
For macroscopic events, the effect of the interaction between the object and measuring apparatus
is so small that it can be ignored. This is not
so for the microscopic elements, however, because
of the magnitudes of subatomic elements.

According to Henry Margenau, there is a
distinction in quantum mechanics between the
preparation of a state and measurement, whereas
in classical mechanics no such distinction is made.
It is the preparation of a state, not the act of
measurement, which gives rise to the uncertainty
relations. In other words, preparation converts
an unprepared state to an "eigenstate" with or
without a measurement; the latter simply produces
a numerical value. Measurement does not produce
an eigenstate; it, as a matter of fact, destroys
the state or system.[21]

This "interaction" is of significance to
knowledge acquisition. The ancient question of
how trees and rocks behave when not being observed
is interesting and perhaps is unanswerable.

Questions of this sort, however, are of no use to
us for it is not a possible source of knowledge.
What concerns us is how we know their behavior
through our active operations. One may, of course,
contend that measurement of interaction is actually
a special *kind* of measurement. This is quite true,
but quantum mechanics brings us a unique condition
of knowledge acquisition——human intervention.

The indeterminateness of quantum mechanics
has been a controversial issue among physicists
and philosophers of science. It has been contended
that the uncertainty relations are not an inductive
conclusion (i.e., from experimental facts) but a
logical inference drawn from Heisenberg's principle
——a consequence based on the assumptions of quantum
theory. Part of the confusion with respect to the
indeterminateness stems from the use of the language
of classical mechanics to describe subatomic elements
as "particles" or "waves" in spatiotemporal terms——
a matter of analogy. The analogy is only partial,
since, strictly speaking, electrons, protons, and
so on, are not particles or waves in the familiar
senses of classical mechanics, where these terms
are used to denote a particle always having a
determinate position and simultaneously a determinate
momentum; as such, both can be measured with
precision.

In any event, we must modify, methodologically,
the notion that quantum mechanics by nature is
indeterministic.[22] To begin with, classical
mechanics and quantum mechanics define the state
of a system in different ways. Although quantum

mechanics does not provide a state description in
terms of both positions and momenta of the variables
belonging to the system, it is deterministic with
respect to its own state description via the "Psi
function." This Psi function must satisfy the
fundamental wave equation of the system. The
square of the amplitude of Psi (not the Psi function),
however, is interpreted as a probability distribution
function for elementary constituents in a subatomic
system. It is in this sense exactly that the
theoretical state of a system under quantum mechanics
contains a statistical component. When the assumptions of *a theory* have a probabilistic or statistical
content, it is only natural that conclusions or
inferences deduced from them will also have a
statistical element. In other words, since the
square of Psi's absolute value is interpreted as a
probability distribution function, then any interpretation associated with the Psi function is
necessarily a statistical one. This may be due to
the fact that quantum mechanics, in its present
state, cannot predict the detailed individual
behaviors of subatomic elements. This does not
necessarily mean, however, that the behavior of
such subatomic elements is inherently indeterministic. It is, therefore, quite possible that
the theory is at present incomplete and that it
might someday be replaced by a nonstatistical
theory in explaining and predicting the detailed
behavior of the subatomic elements. In brief,
quantum mechanics by virtue of its own coherent

theory cannot be characterized as indeterministic.
It is the detailed behaviors of the subatomic
elements which are postulated by the theory through
complex mathematical manipulations as indeterministic.

The quantum concept, particularly in terms of
its probabilistic or indeterministic property
arising from the interaction of the observed and
the observer, may have significant relevance to
measurement in accounting. In the first place the
accountant's activities are very much a part of
the accounting system. What events are to be
observed and how they are to be measured are, in
part at least, affected by the accountant's intervention in terms of his observation, capability,
experience, preference, and judgment. In the
second place, the two basic subject matters of the
accounting discipline—asset measurement and income
determination—are so interrelated that an isolation
of one from the other would certainly result in
meaningless analysis of business activities. This
can easily be seen, for instance, either from the
interrelatedness of the balance sheet and the
income statement or, what amounts to the same
thing, the necessity of analyzing the interplay of
stocks and flows. Except in an arbitrary or
postulational manner, *it is neither possible nor*
meaningful in theory to observe and measure,
simultaneously, the position and movement of scarce
resources with precision. In other words, these
two crucial variables of the accounting model
interact continuously and their periodic discontinuity
is largely caused by the accountant's intervention.

In the third place, since measurement is, at most,
an approximation, the application of nondeterministic
measures or quantum ranges is not only unavoidable
but may be more meaningful and informative, particularl
in light of the dynamic state of the business world.[23]
Finally, although we do not really know the detailed
relations between microscopic elements and macroscopic
phenomena, it may be true, at least from observation
or experience, that there is an uncertainty or
unpredictable element in detailed human behavior at
the microscopic level. In other words, it may not
be possible to predict *specific* instances of human
activities. Whether a macroscopic phenomenon can
be explained fully in terms of its components, or
whether there is more to it than the aggregated
relations of its components, is a matter which has
been vigorously debated in philosophy and systems
theory.

Theoretical Constructs, Definitions, and Measurement
     The act of a measurement is to produce a
numerical value or number representing a measured
object or property on a one-to-one correspondence
basis. The meaningfulness of the number depends
upon how close it is to reflecting the object and
its relations to the numbers corresponding with other
relevant measured objects. This means in general
terms that for measurement purposes, the object
of a given discipline must first be identified and
defined precisely in accordance with a systematically
predetermined frame of reference of the discipline
in question, so that the essence and the operating

capcaity of the objects are known to us before
measurements are performed. In other words, the
output of measurements can be interpreted meaningfully only in the light of such a frame of reference.
What we are trying to emphasize is that measurement
itself is merely an operating process and that
without the guidance of a given theory, it simply
becomes a meaningless act. This is well put by C.
West Churchman who says: "...The important thing
about measurement is not quantification. The
essence of measurement is the very refined relationship
between theory and observation."[24]

That measurement itself is, in essence, a
mathematical description explains only one of the
two basic ingredients of measurement—the logical
and functional relations of the measured objects.
The other is the "content" of the measured object.
As we know, the foundation of mathematics is logic,
and both mathematics and logic employ only analytic
propositions (tautologies) without contents. Their
power and elegance lie in the fact that they are at
present the most highly organized sciences for
revealing the functional relations between elements
or terms symbolically. As long as we can satisfy
this kind of mathematical requirement, mathematics
becomes a powerful tool for us. For an empirical
discipline, however, we need something more, and
this "something more" is the "content" of the
elements. This content must come from outside the
mathematically constructed system. It comes
initially from sense data; and through the process
of abstraction, we acquire, in a systematic way,

a set of basic concepts about a certain class of
phenomena of the world in which we live. Mathematics
alone does not lead us directly to the empirical
world.

We need to know first the essence of the
objects to be measured and to have them precisely
defined. While there are various types of
definition, two will be noted here — constitutive
and operational. The former is more conceptual
than the latter in the sense that it captures the
essence of the defined object; the latter, a
product of operationalism, relates the theoretical
characteristics of a concept to the world of
experience with emphasis on its capacity for subsequent operations. Although operationalism is
undoubtedly a powerful mode of thought in contemporary
sciences, both physical and social, we must avoid
the fallacy that operational definitions are derived
from the operation of measurement. To follow this
line of thinking would be like putting the buggy
before the horse. We are of the opinion that an
object must first be defined constitutively, by
which we then can determine its operating capacity.
In other words, constitutive definitions are so
fundamental that without them operational definitions
will limit our understanding of the phenomena of
the outside world. A good example is the measurement
of the length of a certain object with a yardstick.
With respect to the operation, the state is prepared,
followed by the act of measurement, and the result
of the act may be expressed as xRy, with x denoting

the specific length (in inches, feet, or meters),
R, the relation, and y, the measured object. This
is a "specific" length, however, and it does not
tell us anything about "length."[25] Thus, unless
we know what length is, we will not be able to
acquire the full meaningfulness of the performance,
no matter how operationally the object in question
is defined.

Another crucial point in connection with
operational definitions is that there are a large
number of basic concepts of physical magnitudes
which are not operationally definable, such as length,
mass, and temperature, when "they enter into the
mathematical formulation of physical laws."[26]
Yet, they must have operational capacity to have any
physical significance. In addition, operational
definitions are not always expressible in observational terms. Indeed, many properties of a given
concept may not be subject to direct observation.
It is unfortunate that many empirically oriented
people consider "operational" as synonymous with
"empirical" or "observational"; it is not. Quantum
mechanics, for instance, is certainly operational,
but its scheme is expressed not in observational
but in highly abstract terms of mathematical
equations. The essence of operational definitions
is that they set forth the operational capacity
for subsequent manipulations or experiments, and
the prerequisite for an observational import is
not only unnecessary but sometimes not possible
at the time when the objects or concepts are defined.
Indeed, as is often the case, many of the implications

of an operational concept are deduced or calculated
propositions whose operational capacities are
subject to both *time* and technological constraints.

Save for what has been said about the relevance
of constitutive definitions to measurement, it may
seem at the surface that measurement will largely
have the use of operationally defined concepts,
particularly in light of the basic theme of
operationalism. Upon closer examination, however,
we see that the distinction between theoretical
definition and operational definition is often a
tenuous one. The purity of either type of definition
is almost always a relative matter. Furthermore,
an extremely high degree of operativeness will render
the magnitude of measurement almost meaningless in
a frame of reference because of the narrowness in
application. A good example is the income concept
in accounting, which may be defined in a highly
constitutive way (e.g., psychic income) or in an
almost purely operational way (e.g., cash income).
Neither is meaningful to the accounting operations
at the present time.

*Measurement in Accounting and Some of Its Basic
Problems*

Although accounting has often been regarded
as a measurement discipline, it does not mean, at
present, that accounting *is* such a discipline in
a scientific sense. There are steps to go through
and problems to be resolved before we can regard
accounting as a measurement discipline. The steps
and problems that we have in mind are at two

different levels—theoretical and technical, and we
are most concerned with the theoretical phase of
measurement. This is so, simply because the objects
of accounting to be measured must be identified,
defined, and explicated in accordance with a coherent
set of predetermined theoretical constructs of the
accounting discipline before actual measurement
takes place. This is the same point raised and
discussed previously—that a theoretical framework
precedes measurement. In other words, without a
theoretical frame of reference, measurement in
accounting will remain a mechanical operation without
meaning.

Broadly speaking, the subject matter of accounting
involves the interaction between the human being and
scarce resources of specific entities. Thus, the
motivation and behavior of the groups of people
involved and the interplay of stocks and flows,
together with the consequential socioeconomic effects
upon the individual members and groups of the society,
are the basic variables of accounting events. With
such a complicated class of accounting events, it is,
to say the least, no small order to formulate a set
of basic accounting concepts and to identify and
define, in a precise manner, the objects of accounting
to be measured. It may be noted that although a
conceptual framework provides a sound basis for
measurement, it does not necessarily guarantee
measurement. As a matter of fact, it may not say
anything about measurement at all. Its operating
capacity is to be defined as a subsequent step.
This is a very crucial point, for otherwise the

conceptual framework would be no more than a set
of operating rules for meeting the specific
requirements of measurement.

The preceding discussion relating to the
essence of accounting provides good clues for the
formulation of a set of basic accounting concepts
and for the identification of the objects to be
measured. Although it is neither possible nor
feasible here to enumerate inclusively the
concepts and objects relevant to the accounting
discipline, it will be instructional for subsequent
discourse to identify, in broad categories, some
of the essential elements or ingredients of
accounting events expressible in quantitative terms.
Basically, they are those which characterize a
specific accounting entity's scarce resources and
their utilization, compounded by both internal
and external socioeconomic factors including human
interventions. With this general statement, we
now can reduce the variables of accounting events
into three broad categories: variables characterizing
assets, flows, and human behaviors, relating to
accounting activities respectively. At the conceptual
level of measurement, we must realize the significance
of being able to identify *relevant* variables and
their measurability—a constraint which is the
concern of subsequent operations.

For a given discipline, measurements are not
isolated acts. They must be systematically related
so that the measured results will reveal, in a
significant manner, the relations of the measured

objects and the classes of events with which the
discipline is directly concerned. This means that
measurements are conducted within a well-defined
system. The accounting system is an information
system. It is both a system of itself and a
subsystem of a larger system, that is, a part of an
entity's information system. The major function
of the accounting system is to gather, process,
and consolidate data of a given class of phenomena
in quantitative terms with an end-product known
as accounting information. It is also a part of
the planning and control system, particularly in
connection with the internal phase of accounting
operations. In the discussion of measurement in
quantum mechanics, a distinction is made between
the "preparation of a state" and measurement. The
construction of an accounting system is analogous
to the preparation of a state, and it is at this
point that the stage is set, whether measurement
takes place or not.[27] A significant implication
of quantum mechanics based on Heisenberg's uncertainty
principle is the impossibility of separating the
observed and the observer resulting from an
"interaction" of the two. The relevance of this
is that the role which the accountant plays inter-
mingles, in a variety of ways, with the objects
to be measured from the very beginning. The extent
and implications of the "interaction" at the
"preparation" stage are necessarily, in a fundamental sense, affected and conditioned by the
accounting framework that is in force. Of minor

significance are the specific circumstances of the
entity in question under which the "state" is
prepared and, to some extent, the accountant's
intervention. What has been said is crucial to
the kind of accounting information being produced,
for the data input must come from outside the
accounting system and must go through a screening
process governed by the three factors stated
above—the accounting framework, specific circumstances, and intervention by the accountant.

Although measurement is, in essence, an
empirical performance, it must be borne in mind
that it is an abstract of reality, which is, more
or less, defined by the observer. Since *total*
reality is not possible for the human mind to
grasp, the degree and extent of the phase of
reality with which a given discipline is concerned
are often a reflection on the state and progress
of the discipline in question. Since accounting
is not even being considered as a social science
at present, its measurement is, at most, in the
category of measurement by fiat, as defined by
Torgerson (but certainly not in the kind of
arbitrariness of traditional accounting).[28]

Irrespective of the kind of accounting
measurement, one of the basic requirements of
measurement is that the resulting numbers must be
additive. In view of the traditional use of a
measuring unit of varying magnitudes over time in
accounting, compounded by the piecemeal method of
valuation, accounting measurement so far cannot be

categorized as measurement in terms of *additivity* and meaningful relations (interdependence) of the objects being measured. In order that measured accounting events can be ordered, transformed, related, and compared, accounting measurement may have to take transitivity, asymmetry, commutativity, and other relevant numerical laws into consideration.

The traditional mixture of qualitative and quantitative phases of accounting operations is an unfortunate stituation. A distinction between them in terms of operationalism is crucial to the success of accounting measurement. Value concepts of a nonoperational nature may have to be excluded at the measurement stage. Alternatively, they may be measured by surrogates, if and when possible.

Another unfortunate situation is the traditional emphasis on the exactness and accuracy of accounting figures to the dollar or cent. This is done often at the expense of the meaningfulness of accounting information. As explained previously, measurement is, at most, a maximum likelihood, and the use of quantum ranges or reliance on probability distributions is not only a preferred but a necessary condition of measurement. In addition, we must remember that a single measurement is rarely reliable and significant. Emphasis must be placed on the average of a series of measurements and on deviations from preestablished standards.

The emphasis on exactness of measurement in traditional accounting has, in part at least, something to do with the *timing* of accounting

measurement. It has been said that the basic
difference in asset and income measurement between
economics and accounting is a matter of timing.
Traditional accounting tends to delay recognizing
relevant events until an extremely high degree of
objectivity and verifiability is attained. This
practice has reduced, significantly, the relevance
and meaningfulness of accounting information. If
we wish to treat accounting as an information
system (defined in terms of significance to receivers)
and as a measurement discipline (in terms of
maximum likelihood of measured results and probability
distributions), accounting events must be timely,
recognized in terms of the basic nature, meaning,
and function of information and measurement.

The "multiple-goals" concept of business
enterprises is another significant issue which must
be taken into consideration in the development of
a measurement framework for the accounting discipline.
In essence, it means that we must develop multidimensional accounting with emphasis on financial
and nonfinancial events, as well as financial and
physical measures.[29] This means that we may have
to go beyond the traditional boundaries of asset
valuation, income determination, and financial
reports.

Last, but not the least, is the matter
concerning measurement rules employed in accounting.
We need a set of uniform rules for measurement
purposes so that numbers assigned will not result
in conflicting presentation and explanation of
the object being measured. One of the greatest

deficiencies of traditional accounting is its
diversified rules for the measurement of assets
and income. Measurement rules must be designed
in light of a given theoretical framework, so
that the employment of the rules in the course of
measurement will make the resultant numbers
correspond, as closely as possible, to the
predetermined theoretical constructs.

[1] Final Report, *Advancement of Science*, No. 2, 1940, pp. 331-349.

[2] Robert R. Sterling, *Theory of the Measurement of Enterprise Income* (Lawrence, Kansas: The University Press of Kansas, 1970,), pp. 65 and 80.

[3] Norman R. Campbell, "Measurement and Its Importance for Philosophy," *Aristotelian Society Supplement*, Vol. 17 (London: Harrison and Sons, Ltd., 1938), p. 126.

[4] S. S. Stevens, "Measurement, Psychophysics, and Utility," *Measurement: Definitions and Theories*, ed. C. West Churchman and Philburn Ratoosh (New York: John Wiley & Sons, Inc., 1959), p. 19.

[5] This point was well stated by Yuji Ijiri in his *Foundations of Accounting Measurement* (Englewood Cliffs, N. J.: Prentice-Hall, Inc., 1967), p. 28.

[6] Warren S. Torgerson, *Theory and Methods of Scaling* (New York: John Wiley & Sons, Inc., 1958), pp. 14-15.

[7] Robert R. Sterling, "On Theory Construction and Verification," *The Accounting Review*, July, 1970, p. 455.

[8] S. S. Stevens, "Mathematics, Measurement, and Psychophysics," *Handbook of Experimental Psychology*, ed. S. S. Stevens (New York: John Wiley & Sons, Inc., 1951), pp. 25-30.

[9] Ibid., p. 26.

[10] Ibid., p. 25.

[11] S. S. Stevens, "Measurement, Psychophysics, and Utility," op. cit., pp. 31-34.

[12]C. H. Coombs, "Theory and Methods of Social Measurement," *Research Methods in the Behavioral Sciences*, ed. Leon Festinger and Daniel Katz (New York: Dryden Press, 1953), pp. 470-533; C. H. Coombs, H. Raiffa, and R. M. Thrall, "Some Views on Mathematical Models and Measurement Theory," *Decision Processes*, ed. R. M. Thrall, C. H. Coombs, and R. L. Davis (New York: John Wiley & Sons, Inc., 1954), pp. 19-37; and W. S. Torgerson, op. cit.

[13]Norman R. Campbell, op. cit., pp. 126-28.

14 From Morris R. Cohen and Ernest Nagel, *An Introduction to Logic and Scientific Method* (New York: Harcourt, Brace & World, Inc., 1934), pp. 299-300.

[15]Warren S. Torgerson, op. cit., pp. 21-22.

[16]The distinction reflects the progress of modern quantum theory. By "quantum theory," we mean the old quantum theory developed in 1900 by Max Planck. By "quantum mechanics," we mean the schemes of calculus constructed by Schrodinger and Heisenberg. Quantum mechanics has improved and corrected some of the ideas and processes of the old quantum theory. In general, the terms quantum theory and quantum mechanics denote the area of subatomic study.

[17]Hans Reichenbach, "The Principle of Anomaly in Quantum Mechanics," *Readings in the Philosophy of Science,* ed. Herbert Feigl and May Brodbeck (New York: Appleton-Century-Crofts, 1953), p. 520.

[18]John L. McKnight, "The Quantum Theoretical Concept of Measurement," ed. Churchman and Ratoosh, op. cit., p. 192.

[19]Werner Heisenberg, *The Physical Principles of the Quantum Theory* (Chicago: University of Chicago Press, 1930), p. 3.

[20]Ibid.

[21]Henry Margenau, "Philosophical Problems Concerning the Meaning of Measurement in Physics," ed. Churchman and Ratoosh, op. cit., pp. 163-176.

[22]The following discussion is based on Ernest Nagel, *The Structure of Science* (New York: Harcourt, Brace & World, Inc., 1961), pp. 305-316.

[23]The idea of nondeterministic measures or quantum ranges was also mentioned in *A Statement of Basic Accounting Theory* (American Accounting Association, 1966), p. 65.

[24]"C. West Churchman," The Systems Approach to Measurement in Business Firm," *Accounting in Perspective,* ed. Robert R. Sterling and William F. Bentz (Cincinnati, Ohio: South-Western Publishing Company), p. 55.

[25]This point was well made by Peter Caws. See his "Definition and Measurement in Physics," ed. Churchman and Ratoosh, op. cit., Chapter 1, pp. 4 and 8.

[26]Arthur Pap, "Are Physical Magnitudes Operationally Definable?" Ed. Churchman and Ratoosh, Chapter 9.

[27]Hector R. Anton, "Some Aspects of Measurement and Accounting," *Management Information — A Quantitative Accounting*, ed. Thomas H. Williams and Charles H. Griffin, (Homewood, Illinois: Richard D. Irwin, Inc., 1967), p. 48.

[28]See the section of this chapter dealing with "Kinds of Measurement," p. 181.

[29]This issue has been, in part, emphasized by Yuji Ijiri; see his "Physical Measures and Multidimensional Accounting," *Research in Accounting Measurement*, ed. Robert K. Jaedicke, Yuji Ijiri, and Oswald Nielsen (American Accounting Association, 1966), pp. 150-164.

7 Systematic Explanations
Fundamentals

One of the primary functions of a scientific discipline is to have a well-defined body of knowledge systematically accumulated and organized to provide a basic frame of reference for further actions or operations. This conceptual framework, whether it is a general one for the discipline as a whole or a special one dealing with a certain phase of the operation of the discipline, must have the ability to explain and, hopefully also, to predict similar events. Such a framework, once constructed, is of course subject to modification, improvement, or even replacement as the discipline progresses. The major purpose of this chapter is to expand further the fundamentals of systematic explanation discussed previously, particularly in Chapters 2 and 4. Specifically, we shall explain the basic types of systematic explanations, the

essentials of model building, the requirements and
extent of theory verification, and the kind of
methodology that are of special significance to the
accounting discipline.

Patterns of Systematic Explanation

A "pure" type of methodological system (e.g.,
deductive or inductive) is rarely possible in most
scientific disciplines. Thus almost all systems of
explanation overlap more or less. Nevertheless it
will be fruitful to identify what appear to be
distinct types of explanation. There is a variety
of models in scientific inquiry, but we shall refer
to Ernest Nagel who, in his celebrated book, *The
Structure of Science*, classifies scientific explanations into four distinct patterns: (1) the deductive
model, (2) probabilistic explanations, (3) functional
or teleological explanations, and (4) genetic
explanations.[1]

Briefly, in a deductive argument, the explicandum
(the explained facts) is considered a logically
necessary consequence of the explanatory premises.
In other words, the premises state a sufficient
condition for the truth value of the explicandum;
it is a tautology. This is logically true under
any deductive system. In terms of empirical
correspondence, however, the question is whether
the premises can indeed set forth *all* the conditions
(so that we can be assured of the universal truth
value of the deduced statement) or merely state
some of the conditions. The latter adds a probable
element to our inference.

Probabilistic explanations are statistical in
nature in the sense that the truth of the explicandum
is only "probable." It may be noted that the
explanatory premises of probabilistic explanations
do not formally imply their explicanda. Confidence
in probabilistic explanations rests largely upon
statistical regularity subject to a margin of error.
One may not invoke causal laws in connection with
statistical generalizations. In practice, probabilistic
explanations are probably the primary pattern of
explanation in every scientific discipline. The
dream,of course, is to move from statistical laws
to deductively derived universal statements. One
must be very careful with this kind of contention,
however, especially in terms of the basic nature
of probabilistic inference and of human knowledge.
Methodologically speaking, we wish to note once
again that the main difference between a deductive
model and a probabilistic explanation does not rest
upon the differences in our knowledge of the premises,
but rather upon the way in which the premises and
the explicanda are related to one another.

Functional or teleological explanations place
the emphasis on the function (or functions) that a
part of a given system performs to maintain or
realize the overall operation of the whole system.
It has been contended that each part of the whole
is supposed to play its role properly so that the
common goal of the entire system may be achieved.
This pattern of explanation has future as a referent
and may be said to be goal (or purpose) oriented;

however, it is incorrect to state that under
teleological explanations, the future (which is not
in existence) causally conditions the present.
The patent point is that the choice of a present
action is determined by one's desire for a certain
kind of future. Functional or teleological
explanations often use such value words as "in order
that," "for the sake of," and the like.

Genetic explanations are based upon sequence
in the development of events, describing how a
later event or system has evolved out of an earlier
one (or how an earlier system has been transformed
into a later one). The employment of a genetic
approach is not without serious difficulties. One
major difficulty or limitation is that it is not
possible to consider every past event in the
career of the system and that the selections are
more or less on the basis of assumptions, mostly in
terms of "causal relevance." Thus the explanatory
premises of genetic explanations rarely state all
the conditions of an evolved system; and, as such,
genetic explanations are by and large probabilistic.

The apparent distinction between the aforementioned four patterns of explanation is illusive.
Scientific explanations are almost always a
combination of the various types with varying degrees
of emphasis. For an empirical discipline, such as
accounting, a purely deductive system is inapplicable,
for the core of such a discipline is empirical
correspondence. In addition, short of complete
certainty, our explanations are necessarily probable

inferences. Furthermore, experience from past
occurrences is necessary in understanding the present
state of a given affair, and hence becomes a
valuable, though insufficient, referent for anticipatin
future experience. In terms of logical coherence
and economy, however, deductive reasoning is a necessit
in any formal inquiry. What we are trying to
emphasize is an eclectic system of explanation.

The Foundation of a Discipline

Every branch of systematized learning rests,
explicitly or implicitly, upon a set of basic
statements which sets forth the conditions of the
discipline in terms of its orientation, functions,
and boundaries. These basic statements serve not
only as a starting point but also as the foundation
of a given discipline. They are essentially a
prescription of certain environmental factors,
together with a number of basic concepts, which are
relevant to the discipline. They reflect, with
constraints, our understanding of a specific part
of the actual world. Both physical phenomena and
human activities reflect a world of facts. Facts
alone, however, are meaningless. We must study
their *relations* in a systematic manner, so that
we can understand and explain the various classes
of phenomena of the existential world with the hope
of anticipating or predicting similar future
experiences.

The existential world is such a complex place
that, even though each inquiry is confined to a
small part of it, it is still not possible to

ascertain its every element or property. This is
further complicated by the fact that many of the
elements are not capable of being separated and
operationally defined. In addition, they are often
in a state of flux. Thus, although the theorist
has the privilege and freedom to select and formulate
a set of relevant postulates and to invent concepts
for his inquiry, he is not without having serious
constraints on theorization.

Although different terms have been used to
denote these basic propositions and each has a
different conceptual connotation, most, if not all,
of the basic propositions of a discipline, other
than mathematics or logic, have something in common,
that is, empirical contents, though in varying degrees.
It is often necessary, however, to include a number
of purely postulated statements (analytical a
priori propositions devoid of any empirical content)
for the sake of methodological convenience and
simplicity in model building. In addition, constraints,
either within or without a set of basic propositions,
are a necessary part of theorization.

Criteria of Guidelines for a Tentative Set of Basic
Postulates of Accounting

In theory formation, the first question that
often comes to the mind of the reader is: How is
a set of postulates selected? A simple answer is
that a given set of postulates is often the result
of the theorist's preference and decision. Although
this is quite true, it nevertheless does not tell
us much about the issue. In addition, "postulation"

is only one of the approaches in theorization. Thus
an explicit set of postulates is not a necessity,
but a matter of choice of methodology. One may,
for instance, begin with defining a problematic
situation and proceed with observation, hypothesization,
and generalization. Of course, some *implicit* assumptions, as to what to observe or hypothesize at the
beginning, are necessary. A major advantage of the
postulational approach is its logical rigor, coherence,
or formality. Logic, however, is merely the study
of *forms* without factual contents. Thus when
employing the postulational approach in accounting,
one must bear in mind that the approach must come to
terms with the empirical world. In other words,
besides the rigor of logic, we need to establish
certain criteria to guide us in identifying that
particular part of the environment for which a
set of postulates for the discipline in question is
selected and formulated. In addition, the approach
must be strengthened at a later stage by the process
of theory verification outside the scheme of
deduction. Following are some of the basic criteria
which may be followed in deriving accounting postulates.

To begin with, it may be said that the selection
of a set of accounting postulates is definitely
governed by the way in which one identifies the
accounting discipline. With various versions of the
nature, meaning, and function of accounting today,
as expounded in Chapter 3, it is quite conceivable
that there will be an equal number of sets of
accounting postulates which differ from one another.

This calls, initially, for a *precise* definition
of accounting, no matter how it is defined. In
other words, the setting and role of accounting
must be ascertained, for a change in the setting
or role of accounting would render the set of the
initial propositions invalid. The crucial step in
deriving accounting postulates is arriving at an
accurate understanding of the environment in which
accounting functions. This means that we must be
able to identify the class of accounting phenomena
or events. The range of the class of accounting
events varies, of course, with the magnitude of
the accounting domain that one wishes to delineate.
There are few, if any, isolated disciplines, and
accounting is not an exception. Thus very few
accounting postulates and concepts are exclusively
designed for, or confined to, the accounting
discipline. A certain section of the existential
world is often observed and measured by a number of
disciplines, though with different orientations
and interests. Accordingly, most of the accounting
postulates and concepts are either borrowed from,
or shared with, some other disciplines. Those
which seem to be the innovations of the accountant
are largely the results of modifications in terms
of the operational capacity of the discipline. What
we are trying to say is that the subject matter of
accounting is not at all exclusively carved out
for the accounting discipline. Accounting is not
only related to, but also is founded on, a number
of other disciplines; that accounting, in a broad

sense, is concerned with scarce resources and their flows activated by human motivations and behaviors brings home this very point. It is exactly in this sense that accounting postulates cannot be regarded as fundamental; they *are* only when viewed within the accounting system in a methodological sense.

As stated in Chapter 4, the most crucial stage of the postulational approach is the selection of basic postulates. An able theorist will see to it that elements of personal bias and value judgment are absent from the postulates selected. In other words, he must maintain an objective attitude. An objective state of mind alone is not sufficient. He must substantiate his position by strict adherence to the rules of logic and by observing faithfully the empirical content of his postulates. Otherwise, his bias and value judgment reflected in the postulate will find their way to subsequent inferences.

The *purity* of postulates in terms of empirical correspondence depends upon the degree of abstraction from reality. A high degree of purity would result in a more general conclusion or theory; and vice versa. Once accepted as valid, for methodological reasons they are treated as a priori (whether or not they are truly the a priori type) in order to avoid circular reasoning and the fallacy of proving postulates.

One of the primary functions of postulates is to serve as a foundation for a given discipline. Other things being equal, we *prefer* simple postulates; that is, we prefer to select the simpler of two equal postulates. This "simplicity" rule also applies

to the number of postulates for a given system —
we will always prefer to keep the number of
postulates at a minimum. This may be achieved by
a precise delineation of the boundaries of the
discipline in question, so that irrelevant (in a
relative sense) environmental factors are excluded,
and by formulating more general, abstract postulates,
but not at the expense of clarity. Because of the
complexity of the real world and interrelatedness
of all disciplines, the number of postulates for
a given discipline is theoretically unlimited. For
a *given* theory structure, however, a set of postulates,
once accepted, is necessarily "close-ended" for the
sake of coherence and consistency. All theories
are subject to revision and modification; which can
be accomplished by reopening the set of postulates
of the existing theory, but this often results in
the formation of a new or improved theory.

Hypotheses —the Working Base of Scientific Inquiry
Unlike the metaphysician who seeks ultimate
reality and the deductivist who operates within a
closed system to achieve logical "certainty" in the
form of tautological statements, the scientist, who
deals with phenomena of an empirical nature, cannot
take a position of complete certainty. The most he
can do is to start with the "if...then" attitude,
and then look for concrete evidence to substantiate
his hypothetical statement. It is in this sense
that the scientist uses hypotheses as his working
base for subsequent operations, and they may be
regarded as conjectures to guide an argument or

lead to theory formation. Hypothetical statements
are, by nature, tentative explanations of a given
situation or problem and are made almost always
with a degree of risk. Although theories are
also tentative, subject to improvement, modification,
or replacement, the difference between hypotheses
and theories is largely the degree of confidence
maintained on the part of the inquirer.

How is a hypothesis formulated in the first
place? It may be the product of a creative mind
or of a genius, of which we know little; but this
much is known—the formation of a hypothesis requires
among other things, a good understanding of the
problem or situation in question and previous knowledge of related subject matters including existing
laws and theories on the part of the investigator.
It may contain brand-new ideas or newly discovered
relations of existing theories; the latter may
pave the way for modifying, extending, or replacing
some of the old theories or laws. Since a hypothesis
is taken as a suggestion or tentative explanation,
its truth value need not always be raised in the
initial stage.

The Formal Conditions for the Formulation and
Development of Hypotheses

As a working base in formal inquiries, a
hypothesis must meet the following conditions:

1. A hypothesis must be deducible, that is,
deduction of relevant implications can be made
from it. In other words, once formed, a hypothesis
must be deductively developed. Rarely, can a

hypothesis be directly manipulated and verified in toto. We must, therefore, draw out its implications for subsequent operations and verification.

2. A hypothesis should provide an answer or explanation, though tentative, to the problem which generated the study. Although this is a very obvious condition, it is a necessary one. Part of this condition rests upon direct observation and inference from known theories.

3. A hypothesis must have predictive capacity so that what it predicts can be verified through, say, subsequent observations; otherwise, we would not know what we are trying to verify. A common fallacy is to have a hypothesis so deliberately chosen that the stated consequences are known to be capable of being confirmed by a set of instances; as such, it is not a genuine test or verification.

Hypotheses are infinite in number. In addition, hypotheses are needed in every stage of any inquiry. It may also be noted at this point that application of existing theories or laws in connection with the formation of a hypothesis (or hypotheses) is on a tentative basis too, for these theories or laws also function as hypotheses. This whole situation is further complicated by two factors: (1) it is not possible to have a *complete* verification of a hypothesis and each hypothesis is subject to a margin of error, and (2) there may be competing hypotheses. Given various hypotheses, how does one, through a process of elimination, select the one that will be most in agreement

with the facts of the problem in question? There
is no easy way out of this dilemma. The scientist
often relies upon two basic rules in the selection
process—simplicity (including generality) and
fruitfulness. It is not a simple matter at all,
however, to define and apply these two rules, and
the selection of the simplest and most fruitful
hypothesis requires, among other things, creative
and skillful operations on the part of the
researcher.

Probable Inference, Verification, and Generalization

No hypothesis can be demonstrated as absolutely
true, for it can never be proved completely by
any number of finite observations. Thus complete
confirmation or refutation of a hypothesis is not
possible (so it is theory). The most we can say
is that a hypothesis provides only "probable
inference," and our confidence in it is primarily
a matter of probability which is increased or
decreased by cumulative factual evidence. By
probability, I mean a sufficient series of similar
events. It is meaningless to relate probability
to one or a few instances no matter how unique
they may be. Statements based on "frequencies"
can be analyzed effectively by the use of the
"theory of probability"—an important branch of
mathematics. With regard to statements about how
certain we are that particular events will occur,
however, we are not so sure about this kind of
probability. Some philosophers contend that all
probability statements can be analyzed in terms

of frequencies. Others, including a number of
prominent logical empiricists (e.g., Bertrand
Russell and Ernest Nagel), have cast some doubt as
to whether this type of probability statement is
subject to precise mathematical analysis (i.e.,
the empiricist rejects the "if a, then b" or
causality pattern of analysis even if it is based
on some kind of unique frequency). In any event,
logical positivists emphasize the significance of
probabilitiy statements in scientific inquiries.
After all, empirical statements are probable by
nature and must be verifiable. In addition, all
measurements are subject to a margin of error, and
the theory of error is a branch of probability
theory.

Verification is the process of checking
predictions against observations or experiments.
One never verifies a hypothesis (or for that
matter, a theory either) directly or in toto. What
one does verify are the relevant properties and
their consequences for the hypothesis. As we can
only observe particular instances, we, therefore,
verify particular *consequences* of the hypothesis.
This is why a hypothesis must first be developed
deductively, that is, its implications or
consequences must be drawn out for verification
purposes. In general, any verification is only an
approximation. With this in mind, let us see how
a hypothesis is verified, so that it can be elevated
to the status of a theory.

Verification through observation is not a simple

matter, and this process encounters a number of
difficulties. First, it is time consuming; we must
allow sufficient time to elapse for the predicted
phenomena to occur. Secondly, it requires the
ability to identify and isolate only relevant
properties or variables of a given class of events
for verification purposes. Since all the variables
of said class of events are more or less interrelated,
plus the fact that there are always some new variables
which were not previously known, the observer may
be at a loss in concluding to what extent his
deductively developed hypothesis is confirmed or
refuted. In other words, unless the *conditions* under
which observations are conducted are specified and
controlled, it is not possible to rely upon the
results of the observations. Thirdly, observation
through sense perception may be erroneous. The question
as to when facts are facts is a crucial one. Finally,
sophisticated observations almost always require the
use of specifically devised instruments which have
their limitations. These limitations will obviously
limit or constrain our observations or experiments.
Verification through reproducible and controllable
experiments is always preferred. This is why the
physical scientist has, in general, an edge over
the social scientist. In the final analysis, we
hold that whether verification of a hypothesis is
made through observation or experiment, no complete
guarantee can be given to the hypothesis in question.
Since there are no final hypotheses, there can be
no final verifications of hypotheses.

The substance of the structure of an empirical discipline is necessarily characterized by verified or verifiable propositions. To the logical positivist, all empirical (i.e., a posteriori or synthetic) propositions are hypotheses which are, as expounded previously, always probable and never certain. The crucial question in a scientific inquiry apparently is *when* a hypothesis can be accepted as a theory particularly in terms of generality. No simple answer can be given to this question. In addition, as we travel along the path of generalizations, we are moving further and further away from the protocol (P) field and entering deeper and deeper into the construct (C) domain.[2] In other words, as the degree of generalization increases, we are using more and more theoretical terms and fewer and fewer empirical terms; at the same time, we must be able to travel back to the protocol domain in a systematic manner by means of a set of rules of correspondence. In highly advanced empirical sciences (e.g., physics), characterized by a sufficient number of constructs and an extensive explication and connection of their relations in the C-domain, theorists of such disciplines are often in a position to develop "new" constructs and theories to explain and predict a wider range of phenomena of the empirical world. Although the validity of these new constructs and theories must be subject to verification, those theorists quite often have been very successful in doing this sort of thing in the advancement of

their discipline (i.e., moving from the C-domain
to the P-domain). Indeed the ability of the
scientists in these disciplines to progress from
existing laws (combined with innovative hypotheses)
to newly discovered law or laws is the envy of
those in much younger disciplines. One must be
fully aware, however, that this kind of marvelous
performance which seemingly rests upon a purely
deductive system is not completely true, for all
of the constructs have their roots, directly or
indirectly, in the P-domain. The secret of their
admirable success is due largely to the extensive
and systematic explications of their empirical
propositions, starting with protocol instances and
advancing in a layer-by-layer fashion.

From what has been said, one thing is clear:
for an empirical discipline, nothing is completely
certain. With this much in mind, let us see how to
proceed from hypotheses to generalizations.
Generalizations are of various levels. In a broad
sense, the whole process of scientific inquiry
reflects different levels of generalization—
ranging from observations, concept formation,
measurements, and constructing and testing
hypotheses.[3] Thus, theories are, in essence,
elaborated hypotheses with a relatively high degree
of generality.

All generalizations are ultimately subject to
the weight of concrete evidence. The extent of
inference and generalization rests upon the degree
of homogeneity in the class of phenomena under

examination. We generalize only the common properties
of a given class of events. Although generalizations
often are regarded as the essence of induction,
not all the premises (or conditions) and the deduced
consequences of hypotheses in an inductive argument
are known to be true, (i.e., to have material truth
value). The crucial point with respect to generalizations which we are trying to make is that even
though both deduction and induction are forms of
inference needed by almost all scientific inquirers,
the former is not concerned with the truth or falsity
of its premises (i.e., the correspondence between the
premises and the deduced theories is purely a logical
necessity), whereas the latter is concerned with
just that. Inductive inferences and hence generalized
statements of material nature must have outside
supports; however, we wish to emphasize the power of
deductive reasoning in the process of generalization.
Extensive reliance upon hypotheses of direct verification or refutation is not only too extravagant,
time consuming, and often inconclusive but, most
of all, limits the area of studies. On the other
hand, pursuing hypotheses through indirect verification or refutation by means of deductive elaboration
not only is economical but, more importantly, enables
us to broaden our investigation and to extend to
diverse fields (e.g., Newton's laws are of this
sort).

As a final note, it may be stated that as a
discipline advances, the *movement* from experimental
generalizations to theoretical generalizations is

quite crucial because the degree of generality of the former expressed mostly in observational and experimental terms is much lower than that of the latter. In other words, theoretical generalizations cover much more ground in terms of explanation and prediction. We conclude, however, that all the truths of science in terms of scientific theories or generalizations are fallible.

Conditions and Methodological Requirements of Accounting Hypotheses

Being an empirical discipline, accounting hypotheses ultimately must be empirically verified, and, as such, they are subject to the ground rules of hypothesis formation and verification discussed in this chapter. With this in mind, let us specify briefly some of the conditions and methodological requirements of accounting hypotheses.

The starting point is, of course, to have the basic nature, function, and subject matter of the accounting discipline clearly identified. This has been expounded in Chapter 3. Next, we must set forth the basic conditions under which accounting is being studied. Such conditions are generally expressed in a set of basic postulates, reflecting not only the basic elements of the accounting environment but also the constraints, conceptual as well as practical, which limit the scope and dimensions of the accounting discipline. A tentative set of accounting postulates will be presented in Chapter 8. This set of postulates will serve another important function—it will

provide a general foundation upon which accounting
hypotheses, and hence theories, can be constructed
and tested. This brings out several significant
points that we should never overlook in formulating
accounting hypotheses. First, all hypotheses
should be made in light of the general foundation
of accounting. Secondly, we need both general
hypotheses and specific or subhypotheses; the
former serve as place holders of the latter, which
are needed for subsequent operations. A subhypothesis
may also be regarded as a submodel aiming at the
formation of a special generalization or theory
of accounting. Thirdly, subhypotheses are either
deduced from or made in light of the general
hypotheses. Fourthly, each subhypothesis must be
made with regard for its relations to other
subhypotheses, as well as to any relevant special
accounting theories in existence, so that all the
subhypotheses are related to one another. The
significance of this requirement is that the
various classes of accounting events cannot be held
as isolated phenomena and that ultimately the
subhypotheses or special theories of accounting
will be synthesized so that a general theory of
accounting will emerge. (This may sound like a
dream, but methodologically, it is a valid
statement.)

[1]Ernest Nagel, *The Structure of Science* (Harcourt, Brace & World, Inc., 1961), pp. 21-26.

[2]For an explanation of the P-field and C-field, see Henry Margenau, "What Is a Theory?" *The Structure of Economic Science*, ed. Sherman Roy Krupp (Prentice-Hall, Inc., 1966), pp. 27-30.

[3]For instance, C. West Churchman distinguishes three levels of generalization: Measurement, the first level of generalization; hypothesis, next; and theories, the third level; with observations as an anchor. See his *Prediction and Optimal Decision* (Prentice-Hall, Inc., 1961), pp. 71-79.

8 Systematic Explanations in Accounting

The Foundation of the Accounting Discipline

The basic nature, meaning, and characteristics of postulates were discussed at some length in Chapters 4 and 7. The purpose of this chapter is to present a tentative set of accounting postulates exemplifying, in terms of the conditions of knowledge acquisition, internal consistency, coherence, contributiveness, and empirical content, how such a set conditions the accounting discipline and its subject matter. An appendix presenting a brief, historical survey of the development of accounting postulates is provided at the end of the chapter. The historical survey is intended to show the extent to which accountants have been divided on the postulational issue, primarily due to their differences in viewpoint on the basic nature, orientation, function, and boundaries of the accounting discipline.

A Tentative Set of Accounting Postulates

The twelve postulates presented in Table 8-1 are selected in terms of environment conditions under which accounting functions, with special reference to the broad definition of accounting given in Chapter 2 (briefly, accounting is a measurement-communication discipline in terms of the interaction of stocks and flows). These postulates are presented in three categories: universal, institutional, and accounting. The classification is somewhat tenuous in the sense that some of the postulates can be listed under more than one category.

Motivation and Behavior — The motivational and behavioral postulate underlies all human activities; its implications extend beyond the domain of accounting. In other words, it is a multidisciplinary postulate; and its inclusion in a set of basic postulates of accounting can be made only with considerable constraint in the sense that accounting is concerned only with certain aspects of human activities.

Behavior, in general, is motivated by multiple forces; as such, behavior may be viewed as the consequential action of motives. The complexity and difficulty of motive analysis lie in the fact that motives are not directly observable; because of this, motives are often studied in a roundabout manner, that is, patterns of behavior are examined critically in the hope that they may provide certain crucial clues of motivation. Although behavior

Table 8-1

A Tentative Set of Twelve Accounting Postulates

I Universal	II Institutional	III Accounting
Motivation and behavior	Free-enterprise system	Going concern
Scarcity of means	Accounting entities	Measurement
Stocks and flows	Economic events and	Unit of measure
Utility	accounting transactions	Periodicity
		Communication

may be viewed as an observable response to internal
and external stimuli, we must be aware that similar
behaviors of different individuals do not necessarily
indicate that their motives are identical or similar.
Although psychologists differ widely among themselves
in respect to the nature of motivation, most scientists,
physical and social, seem to agree at least upon one
important point; that is, there is an intimate interaction between a living being and its total environment.
It is generally held that in terms of basic physiologica
needs and ensuing behavior, the homo species is not
significantly different from any other living organisms.
Thus in the study of human motivation and behavior,
some social scientists often start by borrowing two
biological concepts—"viability" and "homeostasis"—
to explain the physiological needs and reactions of
man. This is followed by extending these two concepts,
often in the form of analogies between organic and
social variations, to analyze various sociocultural
patterns of human behavior.

The biological term "viability" refers to the
capability of organisms to live, grow, and develop.
A living being begins with birth, proceeds to
growth and reproduction, and ends with death. All
living things are creatures of their own environment.
They respond and adjust to the ever changing settings.
Thus natural selection and evolution in terms of
adaption, competitive survival, or "survival of
the fittest," are quite relevant to the viability
concept. In brief, viability places emphasis on
the interaction of an organism and its habitat and

on the effects of environmental changes on the
surviving class of organisms. In the case of human
beings, dimensions arising from cultural forces are
added to their natural habitat. In comparison, we
note that biological evolution is much longer and
slower than cultural evolution, but analogies
between these two can still be made in terms of
environmental changes and their effects thereon.

"Homeostasis," a term coined by the great
Harvard physiologist, Walter B. Cannon,[1] refers to
the physiological process of an organismic system
to control, regulate, and maintain its relative
state of stability. Emphasis is placed on coordinated
responses of the organismic parts to any disruptive
forces or stimuli. When its homeostatic equilibrium
is disturbed, the organism reacts to the disturbing
forces by controlling or regulating them until a
state of stability or equilibrium is achieved. An
important feature of homeostatic analysis is that it
takes into consideration all influencing factors
simultaneously. The homeostatic system is a dynamic
one in the sense that it adapts to changes and
variations and accounts for functional differences,
rather than rests upon static stability or equilibrium.
Of particular significance of this physiological
concept is its property of "mutation pressure"—the
tendency to eliminate or compromise any extreme
action.

The extension of these two concepts from the
biological science to the social sciences reflects,
in part at least, the desire of the social scientist

to find some similar natural laws to understand and
explain sociocultural patterns of motivation and
behavior of the human being. Although no definite
conclusion can be drawn from the extended inferences,
the employment of viability and homeostasis concepts
in certain psychological, sociological, economic,
and organizational analyses of human activities has
been quite helpful. To begin with, we may say that
all human activities are responses initiated by some
motivational forces. For analytical purposes, these
motivational forces, though intimately related, may
be classified into "inner" and "outer."[2] In terms
of "inner" motivational forces, there exist in each
person various kinds of drives arising from needs,
wants, or a state of dissatisfaction (disequilibrium).
These inner drives, whenever they arise, disrupt the
organismic stability and create a state in which the
organism is impelled to react. Needs, wants, desires,
and dissatisfaction take many different forms.
Psychologists have compiled numerous lists of inner
needs.[3] In general, we may summarize the inner needs
in three major categories: physiological, egoistic,
and social. Some theorists feel that it is meaningless
to categorize human needs because doing so would mean
that the functioning of the self (physiological as
well as social) could somehow be isolated by its
components.[4] Nevertheless, we feel that a distinction
between biological needs (such as needs for air, food,
sex, and bodily safety) and egoistic and social drives
(desires for security, identity, acceptance, approval,
new experience, curiosity, sense of belonging, mastery,

success, recognition, power, status, prestige, and
so on) will be quite useful for analytical purposes.

The "outer" aspects of motivation may be studied
through resultant behavior conscientiously directed
toward certain selected goals within a given setting.
Some social psychologists contend that motives and
actions often do not originate from within but are
rooted in "the situation in which individuals find
themselves."[5] According to this viewpoint, the
motivation and behavior of an individual are primarily
affected by his natural and social environment.
Social influences necessarily reflect the cultural
pattern of the society in which one exists. This
process is known as "enculturation," which means that
a given culture conditions and shapes one's egoistic
and social motivation and behavior. The process of
enculturating begins at birth. Within the cultural
setting, an individual chooses from time to time the
appropriate pattern of social behavior, demanded or
expected by the society in question, known as "role."[6]
From this it may be inferred that when an individual
assumes a different role, it reflects a change in
his motive. "Role" in this sense may be considered
as a motivating force. We must hastily add, however,
that "role theory" has not yet been developed to
the extent of providing conclusive explanations of
individual motivation and behavior.[7]

The analysis of motivation in terms of its inner
and outer aspects is rather tenuous and quite arbitrary.
Man is such a complex creature that his behavior is
not likely to be singularly motivated and one
directional. Modern psychologists in general contend

that the motivation-behavior-relation (or the stimulus-
response-relation) model revealing a chain of
conditioned reflexes is a much oversimplified one.
In reality, there is a reciprocity of stimulus-
response relation. That is, in addition to the
stimuli that occurred *before* the response, there are
stimuli which occur *after* the response and which must
be incorporated in the model. An understanding of
this reciprocal relation makes it possible for us
to see a much greater variety of behaviors.[8] Indeed,
human behavior is so variable that no one explanation
or fixed pattern of explanation is possible to uproot
its underlying forces. Any analysis based upon a
set pattern of a priori assumptions about human
motivation and behavior, or upon simple and straight-
forward hypotheses, is not only oversimplified but
may also be misleading. Therefore, we hold that
human behavior is multimotivated, influenced constantly
by the interaction of inner drives and fluid
environmental forces. The ability of an organism
to adjust and to adapt itself for existence (survival),
development, and stability requires a faculty for
coordinating multiple factors and their effects
simultaneously. It is from this kind of understanding,
resulting from both analytical and empirical studies,
that we refute the one-to-one correspondence pattern
of motive-behavior relation.

    Our discussion on motivation and behavior will
be incomplete without a word about perception which
relates to, and interweaves with, the stimulus-response
relation. Perception is a state in which an individual
becomes aware of his environment by means of the senses.

The act of perceiving may be envisaged as a sensory
process of apprehending certain aspects of the outside
world or environment. The process begins with how
the perceiver or observer reacts to a problem, a
situation, or a stimulus by recognizing surrounding
elements. Research in perception reveals that
individuals rarely perceive the entire situation;
rather, they tend to focus on those factors which
they are able to comprehend and judge. In other
words, an individual inclines to perceive only
those elements which fit most his own position and
goals and hence tends to leave out those which are
in conflict with his perceptual judgment. Moreover,
a person's faculty of apprehension is often influenced
by preconditioned and emotive factors.[9] Thus, an
individual does not always observe things as they
are. To the perceiver, factuality or reality is
often a relative matter. It may be noted that
people generally are quite active in the sensory
process in that they not only record data but also
assign meanings to the data. Thus, the perceived
data are actually "processed" or "structured" data.
Communication between persons results only when one
person's perception is so adjusted as to correspond
to that of the other. In general, perception has a
high degree of psychological connotation. The
sensory process of perceiving affects and conditions
the motivation-behavior relationship. A person's
perceiving capacity (i.e., narrowing or widening
of his perceptual framework) is undoubtedly molded
by his position, goals, emotive state, rationality,

judgment, creativity, and prior experience.

Although our discussion on motivation-behavior relation is rather brief and sketchy, the point has been made that with pluralism of motivational forces, behavior cannot be singularly studied and understood. The reciprocity of motives and behaviors characterizes the complexity of *all* human activities. It is in this sense that it is a multidisciplinary postulate. Since accounting is concerned only with certain aspects of human activity, an explication of the motivational and behavioral postulate within the domain of accounting is necessarily subject to considerable restraint. Even with such limitation, however, acceptance of this postulate is indispensable, for it underlies the behavior of the accounting entity in general and accounting activities in particular. No matter how we posit the accounting entity, we immediately realize that we are not really dealing with the entity per se, which is an empty shell, but with a particular group of people within the entity and with related groups of people without the entity. Thus, the term "accounting entity" must be used in a surrogated sense. For instance, the immediate concern of a firm is survival. To survive, the firm must consider numerous environmental factors simultaneously; failure to sustain survival rules out immediately whatever ultimate goals (e.g., profit or utility maximization) the firm may have been set to achieve. The firm is a product of its own environment and must act in accord with the environmental forces in order to survive, to grow,

to develop, and to maintain stability. In this way,
the "firm" may be viewed as an organism functioning
in the pattern of motivation-behavior in a given
socioeconomic environment. All of these phenomena,
however, are, in essence, reflections of the
motivation and behavior of a particular group of
people working together as a team. These people act
as individuals and also as members of the group.
There are individual goals as well as group goals.
These two sets of goals, together with those of
other related groups, are not always in harmony and
must be reconciled and compromised somehow, so that
individual and group goals can be satisifed mutually
and respectively. A businessman has the same kinds
of needs as any other individual—physiological,
egoistic, and social. Being so multimotivated under
characteristic settings, he must find a ground for
balance such that no one particular drive will
impel him to go to extremes at the expense of others.
This probably explains, for instance, why the
traditional a priori assumption of profit maximization
under the theory of the firm has not been fully
substantiated in reality. Although the accounting
discipline is traditionally deficient in behavioral
concepts, accountants are beginning to recognize the
significance and relevance of motivation and behavior
relationship to theory formation in accounting;
without this basic statement, it would be very
difficult to understand and explain the various
activities of the accounting entity.

Scarcity of Means——Scarcity of resources (including

both goods and services) is a natural phenomenon of
the physical world. It means that in terms of
wants and drives there is never enough of everything
to go around. In a relative sense (as nothing under
the sun is abundant without limit), scarce goods
are also known as "economic goods." The mere presence
of scarcity calls for, in one way or another,
rationing of available resources for production and
consumption.

All scarce goods and services have price tags.
Two things may be noted in this regard. One is that
economic goods and services are produced at a cost,
and the other is that there is a demand for such
goods and services. The price tag of a product
denotes its relative degree of scarcity as compared
with those of other products (i.e., its power of
command over other products). Scarcity of means
exists in every kind of society. In a free-enterprise economy, scarcity is the foundation of the
pricing system which rations or allocates resources
in terms of demand and supply and in terms of
efficiency of utilization of resources. Scarce
(or economic) resources may be classified into
three categories: natural, human, and man-made
or produced. Except in a very primitive society,
a combination of these three types of resources is
almost always necessary for the production of goods
and services. In general, the major economic
problems involved can be reduced to the allocation
and utilization of scarce resources and the distribution of the goods and services so produced relative

to virtually unlimited human wants and desires for
these goods and services.

Scarcity has as much to do with accounting as
it does with economic analysis. That management
must use the most efficient method of production
and must make a choice among alternatives (decision
making) reflects clearly the decisive influence
and power of this particular environmental factor—
scarcity. Thus, asset measurement, income determination, safeguard of assets, accountability of
invested capital, control and planning, reporting
on management performance, and so forth, are
basically due to the entrustment of scarce means
by investors to a small group of people, namely,
management.

The fundamental phenomenon of scarcity is a
reality, whether we consider society as a whole or
individual enterprises. Preservation and effective
use of resources are elements of enculturation
but are also a way of life that all living beings
share. The amount of resources allocated to specific
entities is the result of rational economic actions
of choice among alternatives by investors. Besides
the immediate investors, retention, maintenance,
and utilization of scarce means in an efficient
manner by individual business enterprises benefit,
directly and indirectly, all members of the society.
It is in this sense that accounting measurement
of scarce resources has both micro- and macrovisions.
In general, the scarcity postulate sets forth a
condition that influences and directs fundamentally

all accounting activities. The primary constraint
is that accounting measurement is not yet capable
of measuring every aspect of scarce resources and
their movements.

Stocks and Flows—In accounting the concept
"stocks" refers to scarce resources measured at a
point of time in terms of their economic potentials
for a specific entity. Flows of resources occur
over time, and, as such, "flows" are measured between
two points of time. The significant thing about
flows of resources is that they cause the economic
position of an entity to change. Our emphasis,
however, is placed on the interplay of stocks and
flows. Without stocks, there can be no flows.
Without flows, stocks are merely idle resources.

The demarcation between stocks and flows is quite
tenuous, as one rarely can tell when flows end and
stocks begin and vice versa. In business enterprises,
the movement of resources is a continuous process
in the path of the so-called operating cycle. For
practical purposes, however, a distinction between
stocks and flows is not only desirable but a
necessity, particularly with respect to periodic
accounting reports in terms of capital maintenance,
income determination, and other types of flows and
their interaction.

Free-Enterprise System—Construction of an
accounting framework requires, among other things,
an identification of its socioeconomic setting
which varies from one society to another. A
postulate which sets forth the pattern of political,
social, and economic environment in which socio-

economic activities are motivated and shaped is an institutional one. The institutional postulate being considered here has something to do with a society emphasizing the market mechanism for resource allocation, utilization, and distribution. Such a system is commonly known as a free-enterprise or capitalistic system.

In general, a free-enterprise system is characterized by private property rights and freedom of enterprise and choice. Private property rights denote private ownership of economic resources protected, honored, and restricted by the legal framework of the society. These rights underlie legal contracts, grant freedom to private persons (natural or artificial) to acquire, control, use, and dispose of privately owned resources within legal limits. Freedom of enterprise and choice refers to the freedom of obtaining economic resources, a high degree of mobility of factors of production, free employment, and the freedom of consumer choice. The underlying driving force of a free-enterprise system or capitalism is the urge to promote one's self-interest. It is under this basic motive that each economic unit acts and reacts in terms of what is best for itself. This indicates that, among other things, capitalism is a profit-oriented system; but it also bears the costs of free choice and use of resources, namely, risk taking on the part of individual economic units and social costs resulting from promoting one's self-interest at the expense of society.

Capitalism is also a market economy in the
sense that it operates under a system of markets.
The market is the local place where buyers and
sellers behave in accordance with the forces of
demand and supply which determine the relative
values of scarce resources. The basic mechanism
of capitalism is the price system, through which
the individual economic units render decisions as
to what goods and services the economy should
produce, how the society's resources are allocated,
how production can take place efficiently, and how
the goods and services so produced are distributed
to the members of the society.

Pure capitalistic economy or laissez faire
capitalism is rare, if it ever existed, in reality.
All the present day capitalistic economies are
mixed systems in varying degrees, that is, a mixture
of government control and restricted market competition
The economic role of government in a mixed economy
is difficult to evaluate. In general, the government
in such a system tends to preserve private enterprise,
to promote competition, to guide allocation of
resources and production in order to achieve certain
social and economic goals, to maintain a minimum
standard of living for all members of the society,
to control business fluctuations, and to promote
equitable distribution of income and wealth.

In addition to the basic features of a free-
enterprise system as stated above, there are several
characteristics which are common to all developed
economies, such as an advanced state of technology,

extensive use of capital goods in a roundabout
fashion of production, specialization, and employment
of a complicated money and credit system. These
features, together with the basic characteristics of
a mixed economy, constitute the total economic
environment of a modern capitalistic society which
conditions or institutionalizes certain phases of
the accounting framework that we attempt to build.

Accounting Entities—The accounting entity is
probably one of the few accounting postulates which
has been recognized by most, if not all, accounting
writers. The origin of the entity concept is somewhat
controversial. History shows that several writers,
including E. G. Folsom, Leon Gomberg, J. N. Brenkman,
and Manfred Berliner, conceived the entity concept
in the 1870's and that Brenkman and Berliner made
their respective claims as to the origination of
the concept in their works.[10] Stephen Gilman asserts
that in relation to double-entry recording, the entity
concept was used by Pacioli in 1494.[11] Despite its
early origin, plus the fact that it has been pretty
well expounded by a sizable number of noted accounting
scholars during the past fifty years, the traditional
version of the entity concept is becoming obsolete,
particularly in view of the ever changing and growing
business world. It appears that there are a number
of dimensions of this postulate which have not yet
been fully explicated.

Accounting entities are basic economic decision-
making units under which scarce resources are possessed
and utilized. Of particular significance is that

the accounting entity, whether it is a natural
person or an artificial one, is viewed as having
its own identity; that is, it exists in its own right.
Accounting does not deal with *the* entity in general
(for instance, the firm in economic analysis), but
with specific entities. It is around each specific
entity that accounting events are observed, analyzed,
recorded, and reported.

An entity itself is an empty shell and hence
is meaningless. R. J. Chambers defines an entity
as "a person or association acting in a specific
role."[12] Thus when we say "an entity," we are really
referring to a person or a group of persons in
particular; and when we say the behavior of the
entity, we are really referring to the aggregate
behavior of that particular person or group of persons
working together as a team. In this sense, accounting
is also concerned with certain aspects of human
motivation and behavior, particularly those with
respect to acquisition, utilization, and disposition
of scarce resources. Besides the people within an
entity, there are other groups of people outside the
entity who may have, directly or indirectly, special
interests in the entity; they interact with the
group of people within the entity.

These people act as individuals to achieve their
own goals and also as members of a given group to
share the common goals of the group. Conflicts of
interest among the different individuals and groups
are to be expected, but these conflicts must somehow
be reconciled, so that the entity in question will
function harmoniously to render satisfactory benefits

for everyone involved. The association of the
different groups of people constitutes a significant
phase of the environment of the entity which, in
turn, sets forth the basic function of accounting,
namely, to provide, with constraints, relevant
information to all parties concerned.

Although the accounting entity can be of any
magnitude, the most important type is, of course,
specific business enterprises. Of business enterprises, the corporation is the most significant
form of organization, particularly in terms of
resource allocation. A significant feature of this
form of business organization is the separation of
ownership from management which, when extended to
other forms of business organization, results in
another important function of accounting—accountability.

It may be noted that the major function of business
entities is to produce, not to consume; and, as such,
they are "intermediaries." That business entities
under a free-enterprise society are purely profit-
oriented is an oversimplified statement which must
be modified. This profit oriented issue has been
discussed briefly in connection with the motivational
and behavioral postulate and will be taken up again
under the "utility" and "going concern" postulates
later.

Going Concern[13]—The going concern or continuity
postulate is a proposition which asserts that in the
absence of concrete evidence to the contrary, the
accounting entity is assumed to continue or keep
going indefinitely. The opposite of continuity is,

of course, liquidation. Thus in postulating the
status of an entity without knowledge about the
future (future is unknowable), we may have to make
a choice between "continuity" and "liquidation."

The going concern concept was conceived long
before generally accepted accounting principles
were established. In his auditing book published
in 1892, Lawrence R. Dicksee used the "perpetual
existence" concept for "registered companies" under
the Companies Act of 1862 to justify cost valuation
of "permanent" assets.[14] Henry Rand Hatfield treated
the going concern as a general "principle" applicable
to valuation of specific assets (i.e., fixed assets,
work-in-process, and raw materials,) and stated
that the exit prices of individual assets are irrelevan
information if the firm in question had no intention
of selling these assets.[15] William A. Paton cited
two essential postulates of the entity theory in
1922, "The existence of a distinct entity" and "the
continuity of this entity," and maintained that both
were validated from the legal standpoint.[16] A
classical explanation of the traditional version of
the going concern was given by Paton and A. C.
Littleton in 1940 as follows: "Liquidation is not
the normal expectation; continuity is."[17] The
Study Group on Business Income identified the going
concern as a "permanence postulate."[18] Similar
definitions were also given by the American
Accounting Association in its 1956 statement,
Maurice Moonitz in his *Accounting Research Study
No. 1* (although he rejected the idea of "permanence"),

A Study Group at the University of Illinois, and
Paul Grady in his *Accounting Research Study No. 7*.[19]
Traditional accountants have treated the going
concern as an "assumption," not as an entirely
factual statement. For instance, Paton and Littleton
stated explicitly that the going concern

> "...is of course a matter of assumption
> and this fact should never be lost to
> sight in the process of business
> reporting... Enterprise mortality rates
> are high... Further, many enterprises
> are launched which never experience a
> period of successful operation, the
> entire history from organization to
> dissolution being one of successive
> losses."[20]

Generally speaking, under conventional accounting,
the going concern concept is used as a shelter to
justify historical cost valuation and allocation
as well as the realization concept. Except for the
restricted interpretation, however, the relevance
of the going concern to conventional accounting is
not entirely invalid. For instance, the periodicity
of accounting reports is in conformity with the
going concern postulate. One may reason that even
the costs attach and realization concepts pass the
test of the continuity assumption in the sense
that only a going concern can afford the amount of
time needed either to complete certain incomplete
transactions commenced at earlier dates or to wait
for certain future events to occur. In addition,
the classification of assets and liabilities into
short-term and long-term categories is also within
the going concern realm. The compatibility of the

going concern concept and conventional accounting, however, generally ends here. Under the conventional view of the going concern, any changes in internal and external conditions without actual transactions are generally ignored.

The decision to postulate a firm as going or liquidating in accounting theory formation is a crucial one. To maintain the internal consistency and harmony of a set of postulates in a theory structure, we can allow only one of them in our structure, since they represent opposite viewpoints. In the selection of either one, we must bear in mind that the formulation of an accounting postulate must be made in light of sequential inferences relevant to explaining business operations. It will be remembered that the selection of a certain set of accounting postulates conditions the type of accounting theory to be built, Thus, it is quite possible to have alternative theories constructed for the same discipline under different sets of postulates. The validity of the going concern postulate will become quite clear, however, if we decide to build an accounting firm model based on the idea of *continuous* possession and utilization of scarce resources. Certainly, utilization of resources is not centered about the liquidating concept.

A deciding factor of the going concern is the *intention* of the firm in question to continue at a given point of time. Without evidence of liquidation, we may have to postulate. Of course, intention

must be substantiated by reasonable types of
evidence, such as the basic goals of the firm, its
performance, its present economic position, the
manner in which its resources are possessed and
utilized, its short-run and long-run plans, and
any other relevant information that suggests the
likelihood of continuity. Only when a firm does
not have the intention of continuing, or when
evidence does not support the continuity proposition,
do all logical inferences based on the going concern
cease and does a different reasoning, such as a
liquidation theory, begin.

No firm can continue forever, and the length
of continuity into the future is irrelevant to the
going concern proposition. The significant point
is that we are interested in the status of a firm
at a given point of time in terms of its earning
potential measured, to the extent possible, at the
same point. As such, the going concern should not
be regarded as a future concept but as a *present*
one. The unknown feature of futurity is formidable
to anyone. Indeed, in light of the current movement
of mergers and consolidations, it seems that no firm
can safely be treated as a going concern. Being a
synthetic proposition, the going concern is largely
the result of past and present experiences, as well
as of a certain degree of abstraction, which serves
as a guideline for future experience without a
guarantee. Thus, in the selection of the going-
or liquidating-concern proposition, we must weigh
the relevance of measurement to the interplay of the
entity and its scarce resources, so that a meaningful

stream of information can be provided. Firms vary
from one another and are difficult to posit; but in
scientific inquiry, we must look for similarities
of firm behavior. We may reason, therefore, that in
the absence of concrete evidence of liquidation,
the going concern, rather than liquidation, is more
relevant in depicting the *continuous* possession and
utilization of economic resources at the enterprise
level.

Conceptually, the going concern is applicable
to the firm as a whole. At the present time, because
of practical difficulties in employing the total
concept, a firm is generally measured in terms of
its components—tangible and intangible resources
on an item-by-item basis. When the going concern is
applied to the measurement of assets on this piecemeal
basis, it is like measuring each individual tree
without seeing the woods. We will never know whether
the sum of the measured values is equal to that of
the entire woods.

Utility—Given a set of alternatives under
uncertainty, a person will choose the one which he
believes will maximize his expected utility or
satisfaction. An implicit assumption here is rationali⁺
(i.e., rational behavior). The reason we choose
"utility" as a basic postulate, rather than the
usual "profit" assumption, is to broaden the basis
for analyzing the economic behavior of the accounting
entity. There is no denial here that most accounting
entities are profit motivated. "Profits," especially
satisfactory profits, in both ex post and ex ante

terms, are, and probably will always be, a major
motivating force for possessing and utilizing scarce
resources under the private-enterprise system. What
we are questioning is that the behavior of the
accounting entity with limited means, compounded by
other environmental factors, is generally multimotivated, that any analysis on a single motivational
force is totally inadequate in explaining the various
phases of the entity's activity. In other words,
we feel that the "profit orientation" assumption
oversimplifies business behavior, especially in the
short-run and intermediate term and that it distorts
reality. Even worse the profit orientation assumption
being extended to equate with the "profit maximization"
assumption of the theory of the firm. We certainly
admire the simplicity and logical elegance of the
economic firm model, but we must realize that the
economist knows very well that profit maximization
is an a priori assumption and that he uses it in
connection with his "perfect" firm model as a starting
point and as a tool for analytical purposes. For
the accounting discipline, we need a relatively more
realistic postulate which will allow us to draw the
kind of inferences that will stand a broad scale of
empirical verification.

The profit maximization assumption has led
students of many different disciplines (such as
economics, psychology, sociology, management science,
and accounting) to engage in countless analytical
and empirical studies to verify the validity of its
factuality. In general, the assumption has received

substantiation   from neither type of study.[21]
Because of its oversimplification and lack of
empirical supports, most economists, in their
analysis of the economic behavior of the firm,
tend to play down the a priori profit maximization
assumption and resort to some more realistic ones.
Of particular prominence is the application of the
"utility theory" to business behavior. Traditionally,
the concept "utility" in economic analysis is
associated with the demand function in terms of
satisfaction or pleasure from acquisition and consumption of goods and services. It is assumed that
consumers attempt to secure the greatest satisfaction
possible from their limited income or means. The
economist has also observed that, as more of a
product is consumed, each additional unit of the
product will give the consumer less satisfaction
than the preceding unit. This is known as the "law
of diminishing marginal utility." Analytically
and empirically, the extension of the utility
concept to the study of business behavior, in lieu
of the profit maximization premise, by the economist
is a fruitful one. The validity of this extension
has been supported by voluminous empirical studies.
While these studies are too numerous to cite here,
we are assured that whether it be, for instance, the
behavior of consumers, entrepreneurs, or of investors,
the common pattern of human behavior in terms of both
biological and cultural needs can be generalized as
that of attempting to maximize "satisfaction" of
multiple motives, often simultaneously.

Although utility appears to be a good substitute
for profit maximization in the study of business
behavior, the measurement of utility is not without
serious difficulties. The major problem of the
utility concept is its subjectiveness because it is
basically a "well-being" or "welfare" concept. Thus
the question is: How can satisfaction or pleasure
be operationally measured and compared? Although
many economists reject the premise that subjective
utility can be measured in a cardinal sense, the
neoclassical cardinal utility theorists would contend
that marginal utility can be measured in *utils*. The
use of util (unit of satisfaction) as a unit of
measure, however, does not seem to solve the
"subjectiveness" of the issue. Ruling out any direct
measurement of utility, we may have to appeal to
marginal utility and indifference curve analysis
in terms of market prices, quantities, and rates of
substitution. Probably one of the most promising
applications of utility theory lies in the area of
game theory, which generally rests on the von Neumann-
Morgenstern hypothesis that the individual, when
faced with choice among alternatives, will choose
that alternative for which the mathematical
expectation of utility is greatest.[22]

Unfortunately, utility theory, indifference
curve analysis, and game theory have their limitations
in utility measurement, for personal satisfaction,
no matter how it is studied, is a very private matter
and direct comparison of interpersonal satisfactions
is rarely conclusive. Thus we must hastily add that

the acceptance of the utility postulate as a basis
for subsequent operations is, of course, subject to
certain serious constraints. Nevertheless, we
regard "utility" as a conceptual and empirically
valid assumption for analyzing economic behavior
in general and business in particular. While
"satisfaction," like motives, may not be directly
observable or measurable, we may consider an entity's
behavior or conduct and the results thereof, which
are generally observable and measurable, as an
indication of the degree of utility maximization.
Economic Events and Accounting Transactions —
Economic events are a class of phenomena which
reflect changes in scarce means resulting from
production, exchange, consumption, and distribution.
In a private enterprise economy, economic events
are ultimately measured by a common medium of
exchange effected at the market place. The word
"ultimately" used in the preceding statement
indicates that there may be a time-lag, for instance,
between production and exchange. This time-lag is
quite crucial in respect to the timing of recognizing
and measuring certain economic events and has become
one of the most controversial issues on the measurement
of stocks and flows of specific accounting entities.

Although accounting events are basically economic
in nature, not all economic activities fall into the
domain of accounting. In addition, there are a
number of events which may be of concern to accounting
but which are either immeasurable under the present
state of accounting technology or conceptually not

recognized in accounting at the present. We need
certain criteria for setting forth the basic
patterns of accounting events. These criteria
delineate necessarily the boundaries of accounting
activities. Since the boundaries of accounting
are in the process of extending (reflecting, in
part, that accounting at present is in a transition
period, conceptually and technically), it is indeed
not a simple task to determine what these criteria
are. We believe in general, however, that accounting
events are:

1. Those which are identifiable with specific
   entities,
2. Socioeconomic, as well as legal, in nature,
3. Meaningful primarily in terms of stock-flow
   relationships,
4. Measurable in terms of not only certain well
   defined measurement scales and units of measure
   but, most of all, of maximum likelihood,
5. Exchange transactions, or the equivalent,
   including both internal and external entity
   activities, and
6. Neutral in nature and have a sufficient degree
   of verifiable content.

   The operations of an accounting entity are a
continuous process. Because of endogenous and
exogenous factors, values of an entity's resources
are constantly in a state of flux. The traditional
concept "realization" represents specific points
of the continuous process of operations, which do
not really effectuate the economic strength of the

entity; they merely verify certain changes in the
values of the entity's resources. The most serious
deficiency of the traditional realization concept
is its time-lag in recognizing changes in resources,
and consequently the content and quality of accounting
information are affected to the same extent. Therefore
in terms of the meaningfulness of accounting information, it is paramount to extend exchange transactions
to include those economic variables which have
significant impact upon the values of the entity's
resources prior to actual market transactions, provided
these events can be measured in terms of some objective
criteria.

Inasmuch as economic events are a class of
phenomena, they have factual contents and should be
analyzed, recorded, and transmitted accordingly.
In this sense accounting information is neutral and
has an empirical correspondence. Any interpretation
and evaluation of factual data constitute a separate
function of accounting which must be fully disclosed
so that the receiver of accounting information will
not be influenced or biased by the accountant's
value judgment. Users' needs vary and the accountant
is not in a position to determine what kind of input
information they should receive. As discussed in
Chapter 5, it is of theoretical significance to
differentiate the positivistic phase of the accounting
discipline from its normative phase.

Measurement —In general, all disciplines dealing
with empirical phenomena engage in measurement. As
defined in Chapter 6, measurement may be broadly

defined as the process of assigning symbols, usually
numerals, to objects, events, and properties according
to rule. Measurement is not only a process of quantification but, most of all, a systematic way of
revealing the interrelationships of the properties
being measured to substantiate or refute certain
predetermined constructs. Besides mathematical
convenience, a major advantage of using symbols or
numerals, in preference to the use of ordinary
words, is to do away with any value connotations of
our everyday language. (For example, the expression
"He is tall" may have both quantitative and qualitative
connotations, that is, in addition to his "height.")
In addition, the use of numerical scales minimizes
the ambiguous content of a given object being
measured for recording, analyzing, explaining, and
communicating purposes. It is generally believed
that realistically or psychologically, quantitative
information, as compared with qualitative information,
provides a more precise basis for rational decisions.

The acceptance of measurement as a basic
postulate of accounting is simply another way of
identifying accounting as a discipline concerned
with a class of empirical events which can be
reduced to quantitative terms. Of particular
significance is that this postulate requires, among
other things, that accounting concepts be *operationally*
defined, so that subsequent operations in terms of
measurement can be meaningfully carried out.
Although the present state of measurement theory
and technology is far from sufficient to deal with

socioeconomic phenomena, it has been tested and
proved that measurement is probably the best means
available for coping with empirical data. Since
accounting events fall into this category, we hold
that the measurement postulate ought to be a part
of the foundation of the accounting discipline.
Units of Measure — An effective way of carrying out
the measurement process is the employment of
appropriate measuring rods or yardsticks. Traditionally
the standard unit of measure used in accounting is the
basic unit of money. The use of money as a medium of
exchange and as a standard of value measurement has
long been established in human history. Specialization,
division of labor, and the roundabout method of
production are made possible through exchange transactions by using money as a common denominator. The
use of money as a common measure establishes the
exchangeability of goods and services in terms of
their relative commanding power which is known as
"value in exchange." Besides measuring actual
exchange transactions, market prices can also be
used as significant references for "equivalent"
transactions. Since market prices are governed by
the basic forces of demand and supply, they are
expressions of objective values.

Money, however, when used as a common unit of
measure, is not at all without flaws. The major
drawback is that the value of money itself is also
subject to the market forces, and as such, its value
fluctuates from time to time. Thus, this seemingly
neutral unit of measure is in reality not a stable
yardstick. This unstableness has caused serious

variations in the measurement of scarce resources over time. In other words, when the value of a measuring unit changes from time to time, objects or events are measured by a yardstick of variable sizes. Consequently, the measured objects lack the properties of additivity, deductivity, and comparability. The answer to this serious defect of money as a measuring rod lies naturally in our ability to neutralize its inherent instability.

Although money is undoubtedly the predominant measuring rod in accounting, we certainly need other units of measure. In view of the complexity of accounting events, the idea of multiple measures is indeed appealing, particularly with respect to those accounting events which are not expressible in monetary terms. It may be stated, however, that multiple measures do not necessarily mean that each class of events is subject to only one measure. Rather, it means that, when applicable, the same class of events may be measured in a number of ways. This multidimensional measurement undoubtedly will increase the scale and depth of accounting information. In addition, it may imply that eventually accounting reports will consist of statements in both financial and nonfinancial terms.

Periodicity — That accounting transactions are identified and reported in terms of specific periods of equal length and regularity is a convention. As long as periodic accounting information is required by some government agencies and desired by both internal and external users, there do not appear to be any alternatives to this periodicity convention, and it must be accepted as a fact. The seeming obviousness of the beginning and the ending of an accounting period, however, is quite illusive, particularly in the light of periodic cut-offs of economic activities of an entity. Thus, the acceptance of the periodicity is not, to say the least, without serious difficulties in theory and practice.

To begin with, we know that the economic position and results of utilization of resources of an accounting entity are attributable to the entire life cycle of the entity. Periodicity forces more or less arbitrary division of economic activities between specific time intervals and hence gives rise to some of the most difficult issues in accounting, such as periodic allocation of expired resources, matching charges against revenues, the all-inclusive income concept, cash and accrual bases of accounting, estimates and approximations of expenses and revenues, determination of unexpired resources, and consistency and comparability of accounting information from period to period. In brief, we delimit artificially the interplay of stocks and flows by specific time periods. Thus, because of this practice, periodic accounting information about specific going concerns is inherently tentative in nature and is obviously subject to modifications and adjustments in subsequent periods. In other words, periodicity injects an element of uncertainty into the accounting process of measuring

stocks and flows. The crucial issue here is how
to form a sound framework under the stated constraint
to guide accounting practice in the provision of
meaningful and timely accounting information.
Communication— Since it is both a rational assumption
and an empirical fact that there are people who use
accounting information and that the accountant's
role is to collect, process, and transmit accounting
information, the inclusion of "communication" in a
set of basic postulates for the construction of an
accounting framework is quite necessary. In general,
communication is the process of transmitting a
message about an event or situation, in the form of
effective signals and through proper channels, from
the source of the event or situation to a receiver.
Efficient communication requires that the message
transmitted must be duly carried out by the transmitter and fully understood by the receiver. Short
of this will result in loss of information or misin-
formation. The ideal situation would be that the
transmitted message to the receiver would be the
same had he had the opportunity to experience or
observe the event or situation directly.

The whole process of communication is rather
complicated. It starts with an awareness of an
event or activity on the part of the information
processor. (Actually, there are at least three
roles to play with respect to a message: observer,
processor, and transmitter. In accounting, these
three roles are generally played by the same
person—the accountant.) He then must observe,

interpret, evaluate, measure, encode, decode, and transmit the event to his receiver. There is almost always a personal element involved on the part of the processor, especially at the stages of observation, interpretation, and evaluation of the event in question. This personal element can be greatly minimized with a sound theoretical frame-work and well-defined methodology, so that anyone who starts with the same criteria of observation and the same set of data, follows the same framework of reference, and uses the same rules must arrive at the same conclusions.

Communication is a larger system in the sense that all the other systems of observing and processing information must come to terms with it. In other words, of the two basic processes of accounting, measurement and communication, the former is necessarily a part of the latter. In addition, the sign system used in communication requires strict observation of syntactical, semantical, and pragmatical rules so that the signals used and understood by both the processor and the receiver create no ambiguity, inexactness, and misleading effects. A discipline usually has two language systems—the object language and the metalanguage; the former has reference to the objects external to the process, whereas the latter has reference to the process itself and hence is a language about a langugage. R. J. Chambers describes the object language of accounting as the system which communicates financial information and is external

to the accounting process and the metalanguage
accounting as the system which communicates accounting
methods and principles.[23] Although a clear understanding of the distinction between the two language
systems is necessary in a communication system, two
important points need to be stated. One is that the
terms of the metalanguage of a given discipline must
be clearly distinguished from any of their vernacular
connotations. Thus the use of symbols is always
preferred. The other point is that the two language
systems should have an "integral quality" related to
the whole activity of the discipline in question.[24]

As in any communication systems, feedback is a
crucial step in the accounting communication system,
because it enables the accountant to improve the
content of his information to the receiver. The
magnitude and understandability of information
transmitted are, of course, the accountant's primary
concern. Redundance of signs used in any message
is, within limits, preferred in order to avoid
misunderstanding. Because the major format of
accounting reports is financial statements, which
are the product of aggregations, loss of information
is unavoidable. The extent of aggregation of
accounting information is certainly one of the
basic issues currently being debated in the
accounting literature. The meaningfulness and
relevance of accounting information conveyed depend
not only upon how truthfully the accounting events
are depicted but also upon an awareness on the part
of the receiver of the methods, basic concepts

principles, and rules under which the information is observed and processed. In addition, the accountant owes the receiver a full disclosure of the bases upon which the specific events are quantified. In brief, the important issues with respect to communication are whether or not the receiver should be specifically identified, to what extent his needs can be met, and the magnitude of the role that the accountant plays in gathering, filtering, and transmitting information, and they certainly will have significant bearing upon the basic function of accounting and the kind of accounting model (positive or normative) to be built.

[1]Walter B. Cannon, *The Wisdom of the Body* (New York: W. W. Norton & Company, Inc., 1932), p. 24.

[2]Alvar O. Elbing, Jr., "Perception, Motivation, and Business Behavior," *Interdisciplinary Studies in Business Behavior*, ed. Joseph W. McGuire (Cincinnati, Ohio, South-Western Publishing Co., 1962), pp. 159-161.

[3]A typical one is provided by Abraham H. Maslow, a noted psychologist who has made tremendous contribution to motivation theory. He presents a hierarchy of five sets of goals or basic needs: Physiological needs, safety, love, esteem, and self-actualization. According to Maslow, "these basic goals are related to each other, being arranged in a hierarchy of prepotency." That is, physiological needs are ranked first, followed by succeeding levels of needs and ended with self-actualization; Abraham H. Maslow, "A Theory of Human Motivation," *Psychological Review*, July, 1943, pp. 394-395; see also his *Motivation and Personality* (New York: Harper & Row, 1954).

[4]For instance, Theodore Brammeld considers only one basic motivational force, "social self-realization;" see his *Toward a Reconstructed Philosophy of Education* (New York: The Dryden Press, 1956), p. 119.

[5]Karl Mannheim is a representative of this view; see his *Man and Society in an Age of Reconstruction* (New York: Harcourt, Brace & Co., 1940), p. 119.

[6]S. Stansfeld Sargent, *Social Psychology—An Integrative Interpretation* (New York: The Ronald Press Company, 1950), p. 279.

[7]A number of psychologists and sociologists (for instance, Mason Haire, Nelson N. Foote, Herbert A. Simon) do not emphasize "role" to the extent of a motivating force.

[8]This point was well expounded by George A. Miller, Eugene Galater, and Karl H. Pribran in their *Plans and the Structure of Behavior* (New York: Henry Holt and Company, 1960), pp. 6-7.

[9]The above discussion on the properties of perception has been substantiated extensively by numerous experimental studies. To illustrate, we may refer to Edwin H. Caplan's *Management Accounting and Behavioral Science* (Addison-Wesley, 1971, pp. 53-54 and footnotes 6, 7, and 8 of Chapter 5) where three interesting experiments on perception and behavior are presented. The first experiment involved a group of executives indicating that their perceptions were generally limited to the activities and goals of each one's own department. In the second case, Mexican and American school teachers were shown simultaneously pictures of bullfighters and baseball players. The experiment revealed that most of the Mexicans saw the bullfighter and most of the Americans saw the baseball player. The third study involved evaluation of a substitute teacher under the condition that half of the class were informed beforehand that he was a "very warm" person and the other half were told that he was a "rather cold" person. The result of the experiment was that the students' behavior (evaluation and participation in class discussion) was consistently preconditioned by their foreknowledge.

[10]See A. C. Littleton, *Accounting Evolution to 1900* (New York: Russell & Russell, 1933), pp. 93-100; and John P. Laconture, Jr., "The History of Accountancy: 1600-1900" (M. A. Thesis, University of Florida, 1969), pp. 126-28.

[11]Stephen Gilman, *Accounting Concepts of Profit*
(New York: The Ronald Press Company, 1939), pp. 48-49;
also Louis Goldberg, *An Inquiry into the Nature of
Accounting*   (American Accounting Association, 1965),
pp. 111-112.

[12]R. J. Chambers, *Accounting, Evaluation and
Economic Behavior* (Prentice-Hall, Inc., 1966), p. 80.

[13]Partially adapted from S. C. Yu, "A Reexamination
of the Going Concern Postulate," *The International
Journal of Accounting*, Spring, 1971, pp. 37-58.

[14]Lawrence R. Dicksee, *Auditing* (London: Gee and
Co., 1902), pp. 179-184; see also his *Advanced
Accounting* (London: Gee and Co., 1903), pp. 5 and 227.

[15]Reed K. Storey, "Revenue Realization, Going
Concern and Measurement of Income," *The Accounting
Review*, April, 1959, p. 233 and Henry Rand Hatfield,
Accounting, Its Principles and Problems (New York:
D. Appleton Century Company, 1927) pp. 74-75.

[16]William Andrew Paton, *Accounting Theory: With
Special Reference to the Corporate Enterprise*
(Accounting Studies Press, LTD., 1962), pp. 472 and 478.

[17]William A. Paton and A. C. Littleton, *An
Introduction to Corporate Accounting Standards*
(Chapel Hill: American Accounting Association, 1940),
p. 9.

[18]Study Group on Business Income, *Changing Concepts
of Business Income* (New York: The MacMillan Company,
1952), p. 20.

[19]*Accounting and Reporting Standards for Corporate Financial Statements and Preceding Statements and Supplements* (American Accounting Association, 1957), p. 2; Maurice Moonitz, *The Basic Postulates of Accounting, Accounting Research Study 1* (American Institute of Certified Public Accountants, 1961), pp. 38-39 and 50; A Study Group at the University of Illinois, *A Statement of Basic Accounting Postulates and Principles for Business Enterprises; Accounting Research Study 7* (American Institute of Certified Public Accountants, 1965), pp. 27-28.

[20]Paton and Littleton, op. cit., p. 22.

[21]There are, of course, exceptions. For instance, economists like George J. Stigler and Fritz Machlup remain as strong advocates of the profit maximization premise.

[22]The hypothesis was concisely stated by Jerome Rothenberg, *The Measurement of Social Welfare* (Englewood Cliffs, N.J.: Prentice-Hall, Inc., 1961), p. 203; see also John von Neumann and Oscar Morgenstern, *Theory of Games and Economic Behavior,* 3rd ed. (Princeton, N.J.: Princeton University Press, 1953).

[23]Chambers, op.cit., p. 180.

[24]Ibid.

Appendix
A Historical Survey of Accounting Postulates

Accountants, divided as to what accounting postulates are, differ in terminology as well. This divided situation has persisted over half a century. We believe that it will be of interest to have a brief historical survey of major developments of accounting postulates. We shall start with 1922, the year in which a significant accounting book was published—William A. Paton's, *Accounting Theory*.

1922 William A. Paton—Postulates:[1]

1. The business entity
2. Continuity
3. Equality of assets and equities
4. Statement of financial condition and unchanged measuring unit
5. Costs attach
6. Accrual of expenses and realization of revenue or profit

1938 Thomas Henry Sanders, Henry Rand Hatfield, and Underhill Moore—Conventions:[2]
    1. Informative financial statements
    2. Going concern
    3. Legal considerations
    4. Adequate disclosure

1939 Stephen Gilman—Basic Conventions:[3]
    1. Entity
    2. Monetary valuation
    3. Accounting period

1940 William A. Paton and A. C. Littleton— Basic concepts or assumptions:[4]
    1. The business entity
    2. Continuity of activity
    3. Measured consideration
    4. Costs attach
    5. Effort and accomplishment
    6. Verifiable, objective evidence

1941 DR Scott—"Principles":[5]
Major:
    1. Justice
    2. Truth
    3. Fairness
Subordinate:
    4. Adaptability
    5. Consistency

1943 George O. May—Postulates:[6]
    1. Stability in the monetary unit
    2. Continuity
    3. Realization

1952 Study Group on Business Income—Postulates:[7]
    1. Monetary postulate

2. Permanence postulate

3. Realization postulate

1953 Carman G. Blough—Assumptions:[8]

   1. Business entity

   2. Continuity

   3. Unchanged monetary unit

   4. Fiscal period

   5. Conservatism

   6. Cost basis

1955 Raymond J. Chambers——Premises:[9]

   1. Entities

   2. Rationality

   3. Statements in monetary terms

   4. Service function of accounting statements

1957 Committee on Accounting Concepts and Standards, American Accounting Association—Underlying concepts:[10]

   1. Business entity

   2. Enterprise continuity

   3. Money measurement

   4. Realization

1960 Arthur Andersen and Company (Leonard Spacek)— Postulate:[11]

   1. Fairness to all segments of society

1961 Maurice Moonitz—Basic postulates:[12]

   A. The environment:

      1. Quantification

      2. Exchange

      3. Entities

      4. Time period

      5. Unit of measure

   B. The field:

      1. Financial statements

      2. Market prices

      3. Entities

      4. Tentativeness

    C. The imperatives:

      1. Continuity

      2. Objectivity

      3. Consistency

      4. Stable unit

      5. Disclosure

1962 Norton M. Bedford—Postulates:[13]

    A. Guidance postulates (relating to the accepted view of the nature of man, with emphasis on his motives and desires in carrying out economic activity)

    B. Necessary postulates:

      1. Measurement postulates (measuring unit, entity, and going concern)

      2. Communication postulates (financial statements)

1963 Thomas R. Prince—Postulates:[14]

    I. of motivation

      A. Long-term income

      B. Varying classification schemes:

        1. Short-term business income and non-business income

        2. Intermediate measures (17 postulates)

   II. of measurement

      A. Business entity

      B. Enterprise continuity (going concern)

      C. Phenomena: events or activity

      D. Conceptual frame of reference: transaction concept

E. Nature of data (phenomena, events or activity): quantitative

F. Unit of measurement: primarily monetary

G. When: realization concept

H. Objectivity

I. Reasonableness

J. Materiality

K. Others

    1. Classification scheme: natural object

    2. Universal count

III. of communication

A. Periodicity

B. Quantitative data

C. Disclosure

D. Statement of financial condition

E. Income Statement

F. Other reports

1964 A Study Group at the University of Illinois— Environmental conditions and postulates:[15]

A. Environmental conditions:

    1. Scarce means

    2. Standards of equity

    3. Rational and honest conduct

B. Basic accounting postulates:

    1. Usefulness

    2. Enterprises as centers of economic activity for accounting analysis and reports

    3. Exchange transactions

    4. Monetary unit of measure

    5. Continuity

6. Periodicity

1964 Richard Mattessich—Assumptions:[16]

1. Monetary values
2. Time intervals
3. Structure
4. Duality
5. Aggregation
6. Economic objects
7. Inequity of monetary claims
8. Economic agents
9. Entities
10. Economic transactions
11. Valuation
12. Realization
13. Classification
14. Data input
15. Duration
16. Extension
17. Materiality
18. Allocation

1965 Paul Grady—Basic Concepts:[17]

1. A society and government structure honoring private property rights
2. Specific business entities
3. Going concern
4. Monetary expression in accounts
5. Consistency between periods for the same entity
6. Diversity in accounting among independent entities
7. Conservatism
8. Dependability of data through internal control

9. Materiality

10. Timeliness in financial reporting requires estimates

1965 Paul Kircher—Coded concepts:[18]

1. Economic environment

2. Specific entity

3. Communications

4. Accounting modes of thought

5. Logical sets of procedures

6. Observers

7. Users

1965 Yuji Ijiri—Axioms (Conventional accounting as a measurement system):[19]

1. Quantities

2. Ownership

3. Exchanges

1965 James W. Pattillo—Accounting standard:[20]

1. Fairness to all parties

1965 Louis Goldberg—Basic premises (or notions):[21]

1. Activity

2. Outlook

3. Measurement

4. Record

1966 Raymond J. Chambers—Postulates:[22]

The postulates presented by Chambers in his 1966 book, *Accounting, Evolution and Economic Behavior*, are too numerous to cite here. In brief, he provides a set of postulates and definitions for each of the following categories:

1. Individual thought and action

2. Ends and means

3. Environment of action

4. Monetary calculation
5. Financial position
6. Formal framework of accounting
7. Information and information processing
8. Communication
9. Trading ventures
10. Accounting for trading ventures
11. Corporate business
12. Financial communication within organizations
13. Service and governmental organizations

1966 Committee to Prepare a Statement of Basic
Accounting Theory, American Accounting
Association—Basic standards:[23]

The four basic accounting standards of the
AAA Committee are somewhat difficult to
classify. Although, we are not quite so
sure of the intention of the Committee, these
standards appear to be akin to accounting
postulates.

1. Relevance
2. Verifiability
3. Freedom from bias
4. Quantifiability

1. William A. Paton, *Accounting Theory* (New York: The Ronald Press Company, 1922), pp. 471-99.

2. Thomas Henry Sanders, Henry Rand Hatfield, and Underhill Moore, *A Statement of Accounting Principles* (American Accounting Association, 1938), pp. 2-4.

3. Stephen Gilman, *Accounting Concepts of Profits* (New York: The Ronald Press Company, 1939), pp. 25-97.

4. William A. Paton and A. C. Littleton, *An Introduction to Corporate Accounting Standards* (American Accounting Association, 1940), pp. 8-21.

5. DR Scott, "The Basis for Accounting Principles," *The Accounting Review*, December, 1941, pp. 342-344.

6. George O. May, *Financial Accounting* (New York: The Macmillan Company 1953), pp. 46-50.

7. Study Group on Business Income, *Changing Concepts of Business Income* (New York: The Macmillan Company, 1943), pp. 19-28.

8. Carman G. Blough, "Accounting Principles and Their Application," *CPA Handbook*, ed. R. L. Kane, Jr. Vol. II (New York: American Institute of Accountants, 1953), pp. 12-18.

9. Raymond J. Chambers, "Blueprint for a Theory of Accounting," *Accounting Research*, January, 1955, p. 19.

10. Committee on Concepts and Standards Underlying Corporate Financial Statements, American Accounting Association, *Accounting and Reporting Standards for Corporate Financial Statements and Preceding Statements and Supplements* (American Accounting Association, 1957), pp. 2-3.

11. Arthur Andersen and Company, *The Postulate of Accounting—What It Is, How It Is Determined, How It Should Be Used?* (Chicago: Arthur Andersen & Company, 1960), p. 31.

12. Maurice Moonitz, *The Basic Postulates of Accounting*, Accounting Research Study No. 1 (New York: American Institute of Certified Public Accountants, 1961), pp. 21-50.

13. Norton M. Bedford, "Problem Areas of Financial Accounting," *"Accountant's Encyclopedia*, Vol. I (Englewood Cliffs, N.J.: Prentice-Hall, Inc., 1962), pp. 5-10.

14. Thomas R. Prince, *Extension of the Boundaries of Accounting Theory* (Cincinnati, Ohio: South-Western Publishing Co., 1963), pp. 175-176.

15. A Study Group at the University of Illinois, *A Statement of Basic Accounting Postulates and Principles* (Urbana, Illinois: Center for International Education and Research in Accounting, University of Illinois, 1964), pp. 4-6 and 8-11.

16. Richard Mattessich, *Accounting and Analytical Methods* (Homewood, Illinois: Richard D. Irwin, Inc., 1964), pp. 32-45.

17. Paul Grady, *Inventory of Generally Accepted Accounting Principles for Business Enterprises*, Accounting Research Study No. 7 (New York: American Institute of Certified Public Accountants, 1965), Chapter 2, pp. 23-42.

18. Paul Kircher, "Coding Accounting Principles," *The Accounting Review*, October, 1965, pp. 745-747.

19. Yuji Ijiri, "Axioms and Structures of Conventional Accounting Measurement," *The Accounting Review*, January, 1965, pp. 37-42.

20. James W. Pattillo, *The Foundation of Financial Accounting* (Baton Rouge, Louisiana: Louisiana State University Press, 1965), pp. 57-70.

21. Louis Goldberg, *An Inquiry into the Nature of Accounting* (American Accounting Association, 1965), p. 86.

22. Raymond J. Chambers, *Accounting, Evaluation and Economic Behavior* (Englewood Cliffs, N.J.: Prentice-Hall, Inc., 1966).

23. Committee to Prepare a Statement of Basic Accounting Theory, American Accounting Association, *A Statement of Basic Accounting Theory* (American Accounting Association, 1966), pp. 7-13.

9 Systematic Explanations in Accounting

Essence of the Accounting Entity Model

The construction of a general or specific accounting theory (putting "material" in a logical form or structure) requires initially that we have our methodological issues resolved. In the following discussion, any reference to a specific postulate or hypothesis (general or specific) should be taken as an exemplification of a certain methodological issue involved. For instance, treating the accounting entity as a going concern signifies that the theorist must reach a decision in regard to the basic status of the accounting unit in order to ensure internal consistency of the various classes of propositions in his theoretical structure. One may, of course, assume a liquidating concern or simply do away with both, as long as he can maintain this consistency and, at the same time,

provide a meaningful frame of reference. Although
I, personally, am in favor of the going concern
postulate, the issue—going concern—itself has
something to do with the content of a given theory
and, as such, it is not essential in our methodological discourse. The same goes for our
exposition in stocks, flows, their interplay, and
general and specific accounting hypotheses. In
the stock-flow case, it is not so much to show
how stocks and flows are measured but rather to
point out the importance of identifying the basic
subject matter (and hence the content) of a given
inquiry. In the general hypothesis and subhypothesis
situation, we wish to signify the necessity of both
types of hypotheses and their relations in theory
construction and verification. In brief, the
theorist has the privilege of deciding upon the
subject matter of a given inquiry (together with a
set of premises and/or hypotheses, technical details
or procedures, etc.) of his choice or design, but he
is not at all above the ground rules governing
formal inquiries.

Nature and Meaning of Model Building— A Recapitulation
Model building is a necessity in any scientific
inquiry. The human mind in general is not equipped
to cope with the complexity of the physical world.
A model is, in essence, an abstract, in a simplified
pattern, of the researcher's understanding and
explanation of a particular phase of the actual world.
In model building, the scientist follows, almost
always, the "simplicity" rule and the "similarity"

principle. While no two blades of grass are
identical, the scientist looks for similarities or
common properties of a given object so that a
generalization can be made. All models are conditioned by a set of assumptions. Model building
for a young science or discipline (i.e., one lacking
in general laws or theories) can be made only in
an oversimplified fashion, constrained by a large
number of assumptions. As the discipline progresses,
some of the assumptions are gradually relaxed,
meaning theories resulting from the model-building
process will have a wider application. In brief,
we wish to emphasize that in the beginning it
requires a lot of patience to develop a discipline
which has no formal structure. In addition, we
must never lose sight of the importance of logical
rigor and, to the extent possible, empirical
correspondence in model building.

The guidelines stated above will be followed
in the development of an accounting entity model.
It is true that accounting, as compared with
microeconomics which uses *the* firm as its model,
is concerned with *specific* entities, but this does
not mean that a general accounting firm model cannot
be built. As expounded previously, the entity
concept of accounting is a theoretical construct,
as contrasted to "specific entities" which are, in
a limited sense, the empirical counterpart of the
theoretical construct. As such, the entity construct
serves as the placeholder for the empirically based
specific entities. Accordingly, the entity construct

necessarily underlies the general model of accounting.

The Accounting Entity, Magnitude of Accounting Measurement, and the Human Factor

At the outset, we need to clarify the extent of accounting measurement in terms of the accounting unit. Two of the basic postulates set forth in Chapter 8 are the accounting entity and the going concern which, when taken together, constitute the kind of accounting unit with which we are concerned in this writing. The accounting unit so defined, however, is such a complex entity that accounting alone, either at its present state or at an advanced state in the future, is unlikely to be capable of accounting for every phase of the activity of the entity. In this respect, we wish to raise two crucial questions: What constitute accounting events and in what sense do the measured accounting events reflect the activities of a given entity as well as its economic potentials? Both questions have very much to do with the magnitude and dimensions of accounting measurement. The meaningfulness of measured accounting events lies in its reduction to a set of measures reflecting, in a significant manner, the performance and economic potential of an entity in question. Individual entities vary from one to another, but in a given socioeconomic system, it is essential to identify their common characteristics and goals. Otherwise, a general conceptual framework would be impossible to construct and verify. Being largely a service discipline, accounting does not

tell what a specific entity is supposed to perform.
Rather, an entity itself determines its goals, and
accounting must accept these goals as given and
come up with effective *means* to measure the
activities of the entity in light of its goals.
For instance, if an entity is profit motivated, the
accounting discipline must provide effective ways
to determine the entity's periodic income. Thus,
income determination is not in itself a basic goal
or objective of accounting. Without the profit
motivation of *specific entities*, one would wonder
why, in the first place, accounting bothers with
this income issue (or any other similar issues)
at all.

The crucial issue now is: To what extent can
we provide effective measures to account for the
activities of a given entity in the light of its
immediate, intermediate, and long-run goals? This
statement is made with the assumption that most
entities in our complex socioeconomic system are
multigoal oriented. Aside from the fact that no
discipline is large or advanced enough to cope with
all phases of the operations of an entity (including
its interaction with the socioeconomic system to
which it belongs and with other parts of the world),
the magnitude of accounting measurement of the
activities of specific entities depends primarily
upon the capacity of its conceptual and technical
frameworks at a given point of time. An acceptance
of the multigoal assumption does not mean that
accounting in its present condition is capable of

providing effective measures to cope with the situation, but rather it is an indication of the operational potentials of accounting. In theory formation, it is necessary to start with a simple model, so simple that it may appear that we are going nowhere at the beginning. Thus our initial hypotheses are necessarily constrained and confined. Anything more than this will lead to difficulties, because the advancement of our discipline depends primarily upon continuous accumulation and connection of well-conceived accounting *constructs* through painstaking research efforts.

In brief, the hope of formulating a theoretical framework with a wide range of application (in terms of explanation and prediction) is contingent upon our ability to build up the C-domain of the accounting discipline. The fact that the accountant is busy making specific, and sometimes conflicting, rules geared to *particulars* reflects unmistakably that he is deeply in the P-field dealing largely with specific instances and is methodologically in a hopeless position.

The accounting model used in this study is an entity possessing and utilizing an allocated amount of scarce resources in a continuous manner. In other words, we are dealing with the going entity. We believe that this is a most reasonable position to take in the study of stocks and flows and their interplay, either at the microlevel or at the macrolevel. Empirically and behaviorally, our interest in scarce resources lies in their productive (or nonproductive) capacities and the results of their being utilized. We contend that liquidating concerns reflect a state of disequilibrium. This disequilibrium signifies a transition period—a period of reallocating the idle resources. With uncertainty and imperfect market, we must bear the burden of imperfect measurement of the activities of a going concern caused largely by the discrepancy between the internal and external values of its stocks and flows due to time-lag.

The accounting entity depicted in our model is a dynamic one in the sense that it changes through time caused by both internal and external factors.[1] In this respect, the two biological concepts— viability and homeostasis—discussed previously should prove to be quite helpful in analyzing the nature of the going concern. A going concern is an entity which moves, adapts, expands, and contracts through time and space. A firm must constantly adjust itself to changing conditions. With multiple goals, a firm must resort to a variety of measures in order to keep going. To be a going concern in an ever changing world, it is far from sufficient and effective to consider only the completion of existing programs established in the past. The past is relevant only to the extent that it has placed the firm at its current position upon which decisions and the course of further actions are shaped. Thus, a firm must modifiy its existing plans continually and what is more important, it must make new plans. A going concern owns and must keep owning scarce resources. This is an endless process and is of interest only to a going concern.

The use of the term "entity," however, is
largely a matter of convenience, for, upon a closer
examination, it is not a very meaningful word to
describe the basic accounting unit. We say this
not so much because an entity is an abstract,
intangible concept, but because of the very fact
that the determination of its existence per se will
lead us eventually to some metaphysical questions.
What we are really referring to is a group of people
within the spatiotemporal limit having command over
an allocated amount of scarce resources with a set
of definite objectives. Thus the behavior of the
entity in question is actually the aggregate
behavior of the group of people in charge, affected
by a number of groups of people outside the entity
who have a direct, indirect, or potential interest
in the entity. It must be noted that this "aggregate"
behavior is a composite sum resulting from an
aggregation or compromise of the behaviors and
expectations of the individual members of the
group conditioned by their respective age, sex,
motivations, experiences, preferences, ambitions,
and the like. To these we may add a number of
factors that constrain the operating capacity of
the entity in question, such as limited resources,
uncertainty and risk, survival, growth, social
pressure, public policies and legal restrictions.
Thus management must *balance* the various motivating
and constraining factors, so that no single force
will compel him to go to the extreme. He is

striving for "homeostatic stability" or a state of
equilibrium that coordinates the various forces
affecting the operations of the entity to ensure
its competitive survival and growth. In brief, it
is the human factor and its interaction with scarce
resources compounded by a large number of personal
and interpersonal factors that characterize the
activity of a given entity. While this certainly
is a highly complicated phenomenon, we must somehow
cope with it in order to gain an insight into the
general behavior of the entity in question. Questions
such as why an entity strives for survival and growth
and why it attempts to fulfill multiple goals, instead
of a single goal of profit maximization, cannot be
fully or satisfactorily answered without taking the
human factor into consideration.

Essence of the Accounting Model

Despite the increasing complexity of our
economic structure and the developments of diversified accounting thoughts during the past two decades,
the basic subject matter of accounting (measurements
of stocks and flows of specific accounting entities),
significantly, has remained the same. This subject
matter is, however, to say the least, a far-reaching
and complicated issue, for the validity and relevance
of accounting measurements (and hence the resultant
information) hinge upon a framework of well-connected
theoretical constructs of stocks and flows pertinent
to the accounting discipline *and* a set of operational
bases upon which they are measured. Thus the
measurement problem in accounting at present is

primarily a conceptual one and should be approached as such. Tools and techniques borrowed from other disciplines, no matter how refined and adapted, alone will not resolve our basic problems. We need to learn first of all from other disciplines, especially the matured and related ones, how their theoretical frameworks are constructed, verified, and put into operation to ensure meaningful measurements.

The accounting entity model is constructed on a broad hypothesis: the amount of scarce resources allocated to a specific entity is primarily for production purposes, complicated by multimotivated behaviors of various groups of people directly or indirectly involved. Diagram 9-1 depicts, in a general way, our accounting model. It shows, among other things, that the accounting entity is simply a product of a given socioeconomic environment with which it interacts, with particular emphasis on the relations between stocks and flows through a path known as "the operating cycle."

Interaction of Stocks and Flows—The stocks-and-flows postulate set forth in Chapter 8 seems to render the impression that stocks and flows are distinct and that stocks are a static concept and flows a dynamic one. While there is some truth along this line of thinking, it is not very illuminating in the study of the accounting entity model. Stocks without flows (equivalent to idle resources) are meaningless and flows cannot take place without stocks. Therefore, we contend that the accounting model is best understood by an

Diagram 9-1

The Accounting Entity Model

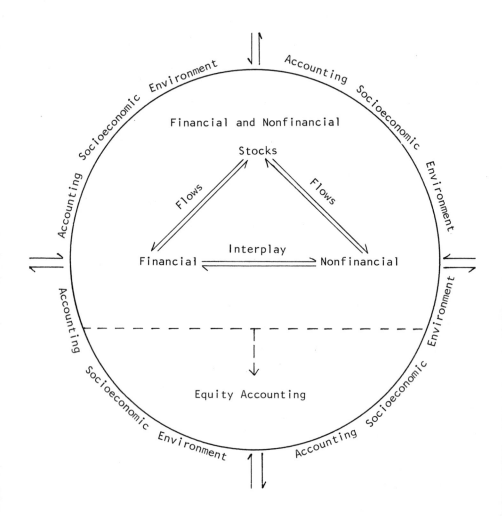

Dotted line signifies conjectural or judgment conditions. See
Chapter 5 for discussion.

analysis of the stock-flow process in terms of
interaction. In other words, it is much more meaningful
to form and explicate a stock-flow concept than to
treat the components separately. Indeed, for a
going concern, it is meaningless to study stocks
without flows or to emphasize flows without giving
due consideration to stocks. The emphasis placed
on the income statement since the 1920's by down-
grading the balance sheet to a residual statement
is a good example of the point just made. The fact
is that these two statements are intimately related
and that without paying proper respect to the
balance sheet, we will never be able to have net
income soundly determined. It may be mentioned here
that an explication of stocks and flows will lead
to such subjects as "stock equilibrium," "flow
equilibrium," and "stock-flow equilibrium."[2] These
economic subjects may be of significance to accounting
analysis.

Stocks are identified by the specific entities
which own or possess them, and the stocks so
identified must be of value (economic potential) to
the entities in question. Although opportunity
costs may be quite helpful for analytical and
decision-making purposes, the gap between the
values of given amounts of stocks to a specific
entity and their market values is often unavoidable,
especially for certain types of assets, largely
because of imperfect market and time-lag.

In connection with stocks and flows, we believe
that it will be quite worthwhile to expound briefly

Irving Fisher's celebrated work on capital and
income which has rendered significant impact on
the accountant's, as well as the economist's,
thought on the concepts of wealth and income.[3]
Fisher's theory of capital and income is intended
to form "a sort of philosophy of economic
accounting"[4] and to contrast and link the ideas of
economics and accounting in these respects.
Fisher's work has produced endless debates and
criticisms by his followers and critics through the
years, however, due largely to both confusion and
misunderstanding of his ideas. Whether or not one
agrees with his theory, the influence of his work
on accounting is quite evident in the accounting
literature since the early days. For instance,
John B. Canning in his classic writing, *The
Economics of Accountancy*, relied heavily on Fisher's
work.[5] Countless references to Fisher's work have
been made by accountants in expounding capital
and income during the intervening years. A recent
critique was made by R. J. Chambers.[6]

Although his followers have developed and
applied an income concept broader than Fisher's,
Fisher himself was mainly concerned with personal
income and ultimate, final, or psychic satisfaction.
Various terms were used by him in developing his
theory which, in part, has caused some confusion
and misleading interpretation. To Fisher, the
term "wealth" denotes all appropriated material
objects including human beings, which are necessary
means to produce scarce and desirable "services"

known as "income." The term "appropriated" or
"appropriation" implies scarce or scarcity. To
appropriate "means" or "wealth" means to own or
to have the right to use it in order to enjoy its
services. Such a privilege is called "property" or
"property right." Fisher perceives the concept
"wealth" in several ways. First, he uses the term
"stock" to denote material objects existing at any
point of time from which desirable services can
subsequently be obtained. Such a stock is called
"capital instrument," "capital wealth," or simply
"capital." "Capital value" is the term used when
"capital instruments" are measured in a common
unit. Income is a "flow" or "stream" of wealth
reflecting changes in the rates at which capital
items move over time. It is an *outgoing* of service
from its capital source—a yielding. If we view
income from the recipient's viewpoint, however,
the service is perceived to be *coming in*. In any
event, it is important not to have "income" and
"capital items" confused. For instance, the fruit
produced in an orchard is not income but wealth.
It is the *yielding* which is dually classified as the
service by the orchard and income to the orchardist.
The same goes for the interest earned on a savings
account. This tacit distinction is crucial to
understanding Fisher's theory of income.

In expounding the process of income yielding,
Fisher identifies two aspects of the flow from
capital sources—services or desirable events and
disservices or undesirable events. The former are

regarded as income flows, and the latter are
concerned with the *use* of capital instruments in a
productive sense. More specifically, he considers
that the completion of every economic event requires
two categories of instruments—active and passive.
The active category refers to those instruments
which are actively participating in the event,
for example, employees and tools used in producing
a certain product; the passive category consists
of those instruments which are being acted upon,
the materials consumed in making the product. The
former is a service of the instruments being used
and is regarded as favorable; the latter is a
disservice of the instruments being acted on and is
considered as unfavorable. He uses the term
"interaction" to describe this double-faced aspect
of events. Thus, there are both a service and a
disservice in every transaction.

This equally balanced interaction, however,
does not result in complete cancellation of the
benefits of the event in question in the final
stage of production, because all cost or disservice
ultimately will be found in labor costs (to the
laborer) and all income or service will be put into
final *objective* uses. The emphasis is placed on
final income or objective uses of production efforts
and on the increase in total utility resulting from
interactions. This is Fisher's way of explaining
the roundabout process of production and of
distinguishing between "intermediate" interactions
and ultimate objective services or "outgo."

Income may be viewed either from its capital source or from the position of its recipient. Fisher is primarily concerned with the former viewpoint in analyzing capital and income. As analyzed by Canning, Fisher follows a "downstream" course in the study of the relationship of capital and income, emphasizing the source of income. Although the accountant takes an upstream viewpoint, being interested primarily in how much appears to be coming to the recipient and when it is likely to arrive.[8] Of particular significance is Fisher's elementary and primary income, which is labeled "realized income" from which two other income measures can be derived—"capitalized income" (or capital value) and "earned income" (earnings). "Realized income" refers to a stream of future services or income, net of stream of disservices over the same period or periods of time. When discounted, the sum of the future flows is equivalent to a present value known as capital value. Fisher's analysis of the stream of future income flows in terms of money valuations is, in essence, a discounted cash-flow study of capital value. When realized income is adjusted for any increase (appreciation) or decrease (depreciation) in capital value, the amount is called earned income or earnings of the period. This distinction between realized income and earned income has caused some confusion and disagreement among his followers and critics. That Fisher insists on distinguishing realized income from earned income is mainly due to his equation of satisfaction with consumption which in turn is equated with income. Obviously, satisfaction and consumption cannot be made from "unrealized" income.

Fisher's model of capital and income is basically a valuation in terms of future expectations, calculated through the discounting process. Thus, his capitalized income, realized income, and earned income are ex ante or expected values. As pointed out by Robert R. Sterling, Fisher's model is quite relevant and effective for decision-making purposes but cannot be accepted as a method of measuring capital and changes in capital (i.e., income).[9] Given the period of time, the discounted value and the present market price of a capital item will be identical under certainty or with perfect knowledge; so there is nothing that is really informative with the discounting process of valuation under certainty. It is under the conditions of uncertainty that the discounting method of valuation is most relevant to expectations and predictions. Unfortunately, Fisher in his capital and income book devoted only the last chapter (Chapter 16) to uncertainty, and he was concerned mostly with the risk element and insurance. He talked about "chances," the value of a riskless return, a mathematical value for a known risk, and a commerical value of a risky return. The basic problem here is that we are dealing with a stream of uncertain income and that any estimation will involve an element of subjectivity. The range of possible outcomes under uncertainty gives rise to the problem of choice and certainly opens the road for alternative streams of income—a pertinent process for decision making, but Fisher did not elaborate the process of choice between alternatives. It may be noted that Fisher's theory has a behavioral base too, as evidenced in the beginning of his argument that the motivation of human beings is satisfaction. He distinguishes between present satisfaction and future satisfaction, noting that the former is preferred. He then equates satisfactions with income and subjective income with final psychic satisfaction.

The influence of Fisher's theory of capital and income in accounting may be analyzed in a number of different ways, depending upon the manner in which accounting is identified. The essence of Fisher's theory is future oriented. Traditional accounting is retroactively oriented and, as such, Fisher's model is inapplicable. The most popular mode of identifying accounting as a measurement discipline also disqualifies the applicability of Fisher's theory to accounting. This is so because the operation of measurement can be performed only upon an existing event. When one wishes to reenact a past event, the operation must also be executed at the present. With respect to a future event, an operation of measurement is simply not possible, if only because such an event does not exist. Even though current value accounting may implicitly have a future referent, it is very much concerned with an existing situation of the

present. For accounting operations, we believe
that it is important to distinguish between measurement
and valuation and between ex post and ex ante
calculations.

Fisher's theory may very likely have a
significant relevance to normative accounting
models (as distinguished from positive or
descriptive models), however, since they are goal
oriented or based on a set of "ought" propositions.
Both goal and ought statements carry explicitly
a future referent. If accounting is regarded as a
valuation process of both assets and income,
Fisher's theory is relevant only when valuation is
made in terms of expectations. Thus the present-
value mode of accounting thought (or "direct
valuation") is very much embedded in Fisher's
theory. Under the conditions of certainty and with
perfect knowledge, market prices are, of course,
identical with the discounted values of future
receipts in monetary terms. With uncertainty and
imperfect knowledge, market prices are, at most,
approximations of discounted values. With these
views, we may have to redefine accounting,
especially financial accounting, not in terms of
"accountability" but in terms of anticipatory
calculations. At the present time, we think that
Fisher's theory in general is most relevant and
applicable in the preparation of pro forma
statements and in certain parts of managerial
accounting. In conclusion, we hold that, irrespective
of the applicability of Fisher's theory to accounting

measurement largely due to its time dimension, his
elegant discourse should aid us in understanding
the basic nature of capital and income and their
essential and relevant properties.

The Operating Cycle[10]—The stock-flow process of
the accounting entity model can be depicted
effectively through the operating cycle which
embraces all phases of the economic activity of a
business enterprise. In essence, it reflects the
interplay of stocks and flows and of nonfinancial
and financial flows.[11] The basic nature and functions
of the operating cycle are common to all going
concerns. A significant phase of the cycle is that
it reveals, in a relative sense, the "permanence"
and relatedness of assets. Rarely can a single
asset function alone. Resources must be combined
and utilized in a total manner. Nonfinancial
assets (for example, inventories, and plant and
equipment) cannot function without the assistance
of financial assets. By the same token, utilization
of fixed assets is associated with the use of
current assets. Thus, to a going entity, current
assets as a whole are just as "permanent" as fixed
assets. The liquidity concept of a firm in terms
of its working capital and composition of its current
assets is valid only in the sense that the firm must
maintain a proper level of liquid funds in order to
keep its operating cycle functioning. Current
assets differ from noncurrent assets primarily in
turnover rates, which are a matter of timing. To a
going concern, there is no greater intent to
liquidate its current assets than to liquidate its

fixed assets. Both types of assets are continuously
on the move in the operating cycle, and neither kind
can be said to be exhausted or liquidated. They
perpetuate as long as the firm stays in business.
The disposal of a *specific* asset reflects merely a
motion of the cycle. It is true that each asset,
once acquired, is on its way to being disposed of.
It is not true, however, when we speak of each
necessary *type* of asset which must be maintained in
order to keep the firm going. The orderly movement
of assets in the operating cycle implies that assets
are planned and controlled by management in order to
ensure continuity.

Income flows reflect the production phase of
the operating cycle of a firm. The conversion of
certain assets into a more liquid state during an
accounting period is only one side of the picture.
The other side is the reverse course of the conversion.
When both sides are considered, there emerges a
process which reveals a revolving cycle of asset
movement of a continuous nature.[12] Conventional
income determination is related to the "liquidity"
concept, mainly because of the realization doctrine.[13]
This liquidity version of income measurement is too
restrictive. The value or economic position of a
firm does not await a particular transaction rigidly
set at a certain point of time. The traditional
matching concept is indeed a severe restraint of the
going concern. Paton and Littleton's "effort-and-
accomplishment" concept appears to be flawless; but
when effort is associated with "cost," and accomplishmen

is stated at the point of realization, it loses its
significance to the going concern proposition.[14]

In brief, we may say that because the
operating cycle reflects the continuous, orderly
movement of an enterprise's resources (both
financial and nonfinancial), the cycle reveals the
indivisibility of asset utilization and thus
portrays the entire course of operations of the
enterprise.

General and Subhypotheses of Accounting

The foregoing discussion of the essence of
the accounting entity is in the realm of general
hypotheses. The complexity of the economic
structure in general and the accounting entity in
particular, however, necessitates an anatomical
analysis of the essence of the accounting entity
model. In other words, we need to dissect the
content of the model in a systematic way. This is
done by formulation of subhypotheses, each of
which must be formed, as discussed previously, in
the light of the general foundation of the
accounting discipline and its relations to other
subhypotheses. In addition, further subhypotheses
may be necessary for each subhypotheses.

Accounting hypotheses are, of course, formulated
in terms of illuminating accounting events. Although
the essence of accounting is related to asset
valuation and income determination, we need a
refined classification of accounting events, as well
as a systematic study of their relations, in order
to build a frame of reference which will enable us

to explain, measure, and predict the numerous
phases of the accounting activities. For instance,
in addition to monetary and economic considerations,
if we wish also to explain and predict the behavioral
aspects of accounting activities, it will be
necessary to have some behavioral concepts and
theories included in our framework as additional
dimensions to our measures. It should be pointed
out that the kind of framework that we are talking
about is a coherent one, meaning that no elements
of the framework are isolated or stand alone. This
goes for any special accounting theories. A case
in question is the advent of the so-called behavioral
accounting, which seems to render the impression
that this new branch enjoys an independent status.
There is no question that traditional accounting is
long on functional relations but short on behavioral
relations.[15] If we wish to look into the behavioral
aspects of accounting acitivities, however, we must
somehow have the relevant and applicable behavioral
constructs connected and *integrated* with our other
constructs. After all, when we say accounting
activities, we are referring to a specific class of
human *behaviors*.

The following outline serves as an example of
the kinds of general hypotheses and subhypotheses
that may eventually be considered in the construction
of a general framework of accounting. The emphasis
here is not so much on what specific hypotheses
(which are theoretically infinite in number) we
would need in the formulation of a general framework for accounting, but rather on bringing our

attention to the *interrelatedness* of the accounting events, so that in the initial stages of theory formation we will not be drifting away from this crucial idea.

A Tentative Outline of Major Hypotheses and Subhypotheses of the Accounting Model:

A. Hypothesis for Behavioral Implications Underlying All Accounting Events

   A1 Economic

      A1-1 Personal vs. Interpersonal

   A2 Noneconomic

      A2-1 Personal vs. Interpersonal

B. Hypothesis for Multimeasure Accounting

C. Hypothesis for Stocks—Measures to Reflect the Economic Potentials of Specific Entities

   C1 Asset Measurement

      C1-1 Single base

      C1-2 Multiple base

      C1-3 Measurement of specific monetary and tangible assets

      C1-4 Measurement of intangible assets

      C1-5 Aggregative Measurement

D. Hypothesis for Flows—Measures to Reflect Movement of Scarce Resources of Specific Entities

   D1 Financial Flows

      D1-1 Capital financing

      D1-2 Liquidity preference

   D2 Nonfinancial Flows

      D2-1 Productive flows

      D2-2 Revenue or income flows

D2-3   Flows related to conservation,
          survival, growth, and contraction
E.   Hypothesis for the Interplay of Stocks and
      Flows
F.   Hypothesis for Projected Accounting Events—
      Planning, Budgeting, and Forecasting
G.   Hypothesis for Externalities
H.   Hypothesis for Equity Accounting—A Separate
      Phase of Accounting Operations

Verification and Synthesis of Accounting Hypotheses

Our exposition on the accounting entity model
reveals that it has a layer-by-layer structure in
the form of a number of related classes of propositions.
For instance, we stated that a set of postulates serves
as the foundation of the accounting discipline and
that a set of general hypotheses serves as placeholders for subhypotheses. We also emphasized the
interrelatedness between the general hypotheses and
the subhypotheses and among the subhypotheses themselves. Now we come to two crucial stages of theory
formation—verification and synthesis of hypotheses.
It is extremely difficult to test the general
hypotheses, not only because they are too general
and broad, but, most of all, because they are lacking
in immediate experiential significance. Instead, we
test or verify the subhypotheses which are, after
all, deduced from, or formulated in light of, the
general hypotheses. Methodologically, the general
hypotheses are confirmed or refuted by means of
verifying the subhypotheses. With sufficient
subhypotheses being made and verified, it is necessary

to have them *synthesized*, so that a general framework
for the discipline will emerge. The validity of the
general framework rests, therefore, upon the interaction and successful testing of the specific hypotheses.

Earlier we stated that, whether deductively or
inductively derived, accounting hypotheses, in
general, cannot entirely be devoid of empirical
correspondence. That is, they must be empirically
verifiable; and unless they are successfully tested,
we will not be in a position either to accept or
refute them. By nature, however, they will forever
remain *probable*—a point which has been made
previously. Although what has been said is still
true, a word of caution is in order here. Among
other things, hypothesis testing involves both
measurements and observations, both of which cannot
be fully and perfectly executed. It may be because
of this that one can never really prove or disprove
a hypothesis. One further point that needs to be
made is that in the early stages of theory formation
in general and in accounting in particular, our
theories are more likely *descriptive* in form and
rich in observational terms. Their applicability
tends to be more or less specific and restrictive,
and their explanatory and predictive capacities
are quite limited. As we progress, our frame of
reference will become more abstract and sophisticated,
characterized by the use of more and more theoretical
terms and fewer and fewer observational terms,
signifying that the framework becomes more general
and powerful in explanation and, most of all, in

prediction. This means also that we will be deep
in the C-field (i.e., very rich in terms of constructs
and their relations) and that we will have extensive
use of deductive reasoning, that is, we will be in a
very powerful position to predict the P-field from
the C-field. Rules of correspondence are always
needed, for we will always have to come to terms
with the P-field, even though we now have the
course reversed—moving from the C-field to the
P-field.

[1]The two terms, statics and dynamics, are widely used in economic analysis; both are borrowed from mathematical mechanics, but the economist has not been very faithful to the original meanings of these terms. Statics is concerned with rest, or more precisely, with the study of bodies in equilibrium (i.e., zero forces). Dynamics deals with physical phenomena involving acceleration. In economic analysis, a static condition is defined as "one in which certain key variables (the quantities of commodities that are produced and consumed, and the prices at which they are exchanged) are unchanging. A dynamic condition is then, by inevitable opposition, one in which they are changing..." John Hicks, *Capital and Growth* (Oxford University Press, 1965), p. 6. In using these two terms here, we shall be as unfaithful as the economist.

[2]See John Hicks, *Capital and Growth* (New York: Oxford University Press, 1965), pp. 80-93.

[3]Irving Fisher, *The Nature of Capital and Income* (New York: The Macmillan Co., 1906).

[4]Ibid., p. vii.

[5]John B. Canning, *The Economics of Accountancy* (New York: The Ronald Press Company, 1929).

[6]R. J. Chambers, "Income and Capital: Fisher's Legacy," *Journal of Accounting Research*, Spring, 1971, pp. 137-149.

[7]Canning, op. cit., p. 148.

[8]Canning, ibid., pp. 161-62.

[9]Robert R. Sterling, *Theory of the Measurement of Enterprise Income* (Lawrence, Kansas: The University Press of Kansas, 1970). pp. 217 and 245.

[10]Partly adapted from S. C. Yu's "A Reexamination of the Going Concern Postulate," *The International Journal of Accounting.* Spring, 1971, pp. 51-52, 55.

[11]For a discussion of the interplay of nonfinancial and financial flows, see S. C. Yu, "A Flow-of-Resources Statement for Business Enterprises," *The Accounting Review,* July, 1969, pp. 571-82.

[12]The two phases of the operating cycle and their interplays were well stated by A. C. Littleton in his *Structure of Accounting Theory* (Menasha, Wisconsin: American Accounting Association, 1953), pp. 80-81, 98.

[13]Charles T. Horngren disputes, to some extent, "liquidity as a characteristic of realization... because it...is subject to too many exceptions for comfort." See his "How Should We Interpret the Realization Concept?" *The Accounting Review* (April 1965) p. 330, including his comments on Carl T. Devine's "realization construct" in footnote 30.

[14]W. A. Paton and A. C. Littleton, *Corporate Accounting Standards,* (American Accounting Association, 1940, p. 14-15.)

[15]This point was well made by Dwight P. Flanders over ten years ago. See his "Accountancy, Systematized Learning and Economics," *The Accounting Review,* October 1961.

Index